Basic Grammar *and* Usage
Eighth Edition

Penelope Choy
Los Angeles City College, Emerita

Dorothy Goldbart Clark
California State University, Northridge

WADSWORTH
CENGAGE Learning™

Australia • Brazil • Japan • Korea • Mexico • Singapore • Spain • United Kingdom • United States

WADSWORTH
CENGAGE Learning™

Basic Grammar and Usage, Eighth Edition

Penelope Choy, Dorothy Goldbart Clark

Development Editor: Cathylnn Richard Dodson

Assistant Editor: Janine Tangney

Editorial Assistant: Melanie Opacki

Marketing Manager: Kirsten Stoller

Marketing Communications Manager: Martha Pfeiffer

Art Director: Jill Ort

Print Buyer: Denise Powers

Permissions Editor: Margaret Chamberlain-Gaston

Production Service: Pre-PressPMG

Cover Designer: Steve Schirra

Compositor: Pre-PressPMG

For product information and technology assistance, contact us at
Cengage Learning Customer & Sales Support, 1-800-354-9706

For permission to use material from this text or product, submit all requests online at **cengage.com/permissions**
Further permissions questions can be emailed to **permissionrequest@cengage.com**

Library of Congress Control Number: 2009941321

ISBN-13: 978-1-4282-1155-1

ISBN-10: 1-4282-1155-1

Wadsworth
20 Channel Center Street
Boston, MA 02210
USA

Cengage Learning is a leading provider of customized learning solutions with office locations around the globe, including Singapore, the United Kingdom, Australia, Mexico, Brazil, and Japan. Locate your local office at:
international.cengage.com/region

Cengage Learning products are represented in Canada by Nelson Education, Ltd.

For your course and learning solutions, visit **www.cengage.com**

Purchase any of our products at your local college store or at our preferred online store **www.CengageBrain.com**

Printed in the United States of America

6 7   17

CONTENTS

PREFACE TO THE EIGHTH EDITION

More than thirty years have passed since Penelope Choy wrote the first edition of *Basic Grammar and Usage* in 1978. She and Dorothy Clark, who has been a coauthor of this text since the fourth edition, are gratified that instructors continue to use our book.

As in previous revisions, the eighth edition includes new exercises for each chapter, along with a few of the authors' favorite exercises from previous editions. At the suggestion of instructors, Units 3 and 4 now include separate exercises that require students to compose their own sentences, using the structures discussed in each chapter (for example, compound sentences, parenthetical expressions, or restrictive and nonrestrictive clauses). In Unit 6, students are also asked to write sentences using parallel structure and correctly positioned modifiers. The section on apostrophes has also been rewritten and expanded.

The eighth edition retains the chapter on composing paragraphs that first appeared in the seventh edition. This chapter, written by Dorothy Clark, has been revised and now includes examples of paragraphs written by her students for users of this book to analyze.

This eighth edition of *Basic Grammar and Usage* preserves the format of the earlier editions. The text contains six grammar units, beginning with the unit on subject-verb identification, which forms the foundation for the rest of the book. It continues with five other units devoted to specific areas of grammar, such as subject-verb agreement or pronoun usage. Each unit is divided into four or five short chapters to make acquisition of the material easier for the students. Each chapter includes clear explanations of grammar rules and structures and provides copious examples for each point. Short exercises for each new grammar point occur throughout every chapter.

At the end of each chapter are two (and in some units, three) exercises. Exercise A covers only the material presented in that chapter. Exercise B reviews material covered in earlier chapters in that particular unit to ensure that students remember what they have previously studied and are able to see the relationships among the various chapters. For example, in Chapter 13 students begin by learning what a parenthetical expression is and how to punctuate it. In Chapter 14 they are introduced to appositives, which are punctuated in the same way. Having mastered appositives, the students move on in Chapter 15 to restrictive and nonrestrictive clauses. This usually challenging topic is made easier because the students can now see the adjective clause as an expansion of information contained in an appositive, and they already know the punctuation rule for separating words that contain "extra" information from the sentences in which they occur. "C" exercises require students to compose their own sentences, such as writing one sentence using *who* in a restrictive clause and another using *who* in a nonrestrictive clause.

To help in holding the students' interest, most of the "A" and "B" exercises are written in narrative form on a wide variety of topics. A comprehensive review exercise at the end of each unit tests the students' knowledge of the entire sequence of lessons for that unit. All of the exercises are on perforated pages that the students can remove from the book. Answers to the "A" exercises are printed in the appendix so that the students can check their own work. Answers to the "B" exercises appear only in the Instructor's Manual so that these exercises can be assigned as homework. The Instructor's Manual is described in more detail below.

Except for Unit 1, which involves identifying subjects and verbs in a sentence, we have tried to include exercises that emphasize recognizing and correcting errors. This emphasis on error correction reflects our belief that a primary reason for studying grammar and usage is to help students learn to correct errors in their own writing, and, ultimately, to avoid making these mistakes in the future. For this reason, many of the chapters include not just single-sentence items for the students to correct but short, multi-paragraph essays that the students proofread for a particular kind of error.

An Instructor's Manual is available to anyone who adopts this book. Besides the answers to the "B" exercises, the manual contains three different sets of tests. Detailed unit tests provide the instructor with ready-to-photocopy exams for each section of the book. Brief, but comprehensive, diagnostic tests for every unit in the book can be used to measure how much the students already know about grammar at the beginning of the course. Instructors who do not plan to cover the entire book can also use these tests to determine which units their students need to study. Achievement tests, which are identical in format to the diagnostic tests, measure what the students have learned after completing the course and may be used as a final exam. (By "identical in format," we mean that item number one on the diagnostic test for Unit One covers the same grammar rule as item number one on the achievement test. Therefore, the instructor can see exactly which points of grammar students have learned or failed to learn during the semester.) These tests are printed on eight and a half by eleven perforated pages for convenient reproduction, and answers for each exam are included in the manual. We suggest that the diagnostic tests be given at the very beginning of the course and that the achievement tests be given at the end. If instructors prefer to prepare their own exams, the tests in the Instructor's Manual may be used for extra practice.

Although *Basic Grammar and Usage* was originally designed for students whose native language is English, it has also been used by students learning English as a second language. In addition to being a classroom text, *Basic Grammar and Usage* can also be used in writing centers and for individual study.

Many people have participated in the preparation of this book. We are particularly grateful to the instructors who reviewed our text and who suggested revisions for this edition:

Amye Howell, *Copiah-Lincoln Community College*
Shiloh Winsor, *Grays Harbor College*
Dee Robbins, *Black Hawk College*
Mary Beth Spore, *Saint Vincent College*
Kathleen M. Fritsch, *Dawson Community College*
Lawrence Barkley, *Mt. San Jacinto College Menifee Valley Campus*
Dr. Ann Marie Prengaman, *Lane Community College*
Pajer, *Gonzaga University*
Nicole Donald, *Copiah-Lincoln Community College*
Kathryn Henkins, *Mt. San Antonio College*
Ruth Ochoa, *Sacramento City College*
Jane Perry, *Norwalk Community College*
Rolando Jorif, *Borough of Manhattan Community College*

We would also like to thank the following people who oversaw the production of this book.

Publisher: Lyn Uhl
Director of Developmental English: Annie Todd
Development Editor: Cathylnn Richard Dodson
Associate Editor: Janine Tangney
Editorial Assistant: Melanie Opacki
Associate Media Editor: Emily Ryan
Marketing Manager: Kirsten Stoller
Marketing Assistant: Ryan Ahern
Image Permissions Acquisitions Manager: Amanda Groszko
Text Permissions Manager: Margaret Chamberlain-Gaston
Media Project Manager: Ronda Robinson
Manufacturing Director: Denise Powers
Production Manager: Samantha Ross Miller
Production Coordinator: Margaret Bridges
Art Director: Jill Ort
Product Project Manager: Prashanth Kamavarapu
Image Researcher: John Hill

Penelope Choy would like to thank the students she encountered during her forty-one years of teaching English and ESL. Their many questions about English grammar inspired her to write the first and subsequent editions of this book. She is also grateful to the instructors at Los Angeles City College who used *Basic Grammar and Usage* during the thirty-two years she taught there. Her stepson, Joel Rothman, who taught her to use a computer many years ago, showed her how to use a CD for this version. For his constant support in every area of her life, Penny is grateful to her husband, Gene Rothman, whose patience and good humor are especially appreciated when she has writing deadlines to meet.

Dorothy Clark would like to thank her husband, Kevin O'Neill, for his constant, loving support and creative encouragement; her children, Julia and Ben, for the inspiration they offer; and her students, for the lessons they continue to teach her.

Both of us would like to thank the hundreds of instructors and the thousands of students who have used *Basic Grammar and Usage* during the past four decades. We know personally the relief students feel when they realize that English grammar is comprehensible and that it can be studied systematically. We hope that your students have similarly successful experiences.

Preface to the First Edition

Basic Grammar and Usage was originally written for students in a special admissions program at the University of California, Los Angeles. As part of their participation in the program, the students were enrolled in a composition and grammar course designed to prepare them for the university's freshman English courses. When the program began in 1971, none of the grammar textbooks then on the market seemed suitable for the students, whose previous exposure to grammar had been cursory or, in some cases, nonexistent. As the director of the program's English classes, I decided to write a book of my own that would cover the most important areas of grammar and usage in a way that would be easily understood by my students.

The original version of *Basic Grammar and Usage* received an enthusiastic response from the students and was used successfully throughout the three-year duration of the program. After the program ended in 1974, many of the instructors asked permission to reproduce the book for use in their new teaching positions. By the time copies of *Basic Grammar and Usage* reached Harcourt Brace Jovanovich in 1975, the text had already been used by more than 1,500 students in nearly a dozen schools.

Basic Grammar and Usage presents material in small segments so that students can master a particular topic one step at a time. The lessons within each unit are cumulative. For example, students doing the pronoun exercises for Lesson 19 will find that those exercises include a review of the constructions treated in Lessons 16 to 18. This approach reinforces the students' grasp of the material and helps them develop the skills they need for the writing of compositions. To make them more interesting to students, the exercises in four of the six units are presented as short narratives rather than as lists of unrelated sentences. Each lesson concludes with two exercises, which may be either used in class or assigned as homework. In addition, each unit ends with a composition that the students must proofread for errors and then correct to demonstrate mastery of the material.

Students who have never before studied grammar systematically will find that working through the text from beginning to end provides an insight into the basic patterns of English grammar. As one student commented on an end-of-course evaluation, "The most important thing I learned from *Basic Grammar and Usage* is that if you learn what an independent clause is, half of your grammar problems are over." On the other hand, students who do not need a total review of grammar can concentrate on the specific areas in which they have weaknesses. To help the instructor evaluate both types of student, the Instructor's Manual accompanying the text

xi

includes a diagnostic test and a post-test divided into sections corresponding to the units in the book. There are also separate achievement tests for each unit, as well as answer keys to the exercises presented in the text.

Although *Basic Grammar and Usage* is designed for students whose native language is English, it has been used successfully by students learning English as a second language. In addition to being a classroom text, *Basic Grammar and Usage* can be used in writing labs and for individual tutoring.

Many people have shared in the preparation of *Basic Grammar and Usage*. I wish in particular to thank the instructors and administrators of UCLA's Academic Advancement Program, where this book originated. In revising the text for publication, I have been greatly helped by the suggestions of Regina Sackmary of Queensborough Community College of the City University of New York and by Elizabeth Gavin, formerly of California State University, Long Beach, who reviewed the manuscript for me. Sue Houchins of the Black Studies Center of the Claremont Colleges contributed many ideas and reference materials for the exercises. An author could not ask for more supportive people to work with than the staff of Harcourt Brace Jovanovich. I owe a special debt of gratitude to Raoul Savoie, who first brought the UCLA version of the text to the attention of his company. I also wish to thank Lauren Procton, who was responsible for the editing, and Eben W. Ludlow, who has provided guidance and encouragement throughout all the stages of this book's development.

Penelope Choy

UNIT 1

IDENTIFYING SUBJECTS
AND VERBS

C H A P T E R

1

SENTENCES WITH ONE SUBJECT AND ONE VERB

Aakriti Kundal

The most important grammatical skill you can learn is how to identify subjects and verbs. Just as solving arithmetic problems requires that you know the multiplication tables perfectly, solving grammatical problems requires you to identify subjects and verbs with perfect accuracy. This is not as difficult as it may sound. With practice, recognizing subjects and verbs will become as automatic as knowing that $2 + 2 = 4$.

Although in conversation people often speak in short word groups that may not be complete sentences, in writing it is customary to use complete sentences.

A complete sentence contains at least one subject and one verb.

A sentence can be thought of as a statement describing an *actor* performing a particular *action*. For example, in the sentence "The dog ran," the *actor* or person performing the action is the dog. What *action* did the dog perform? He *ran*. This *actor–action* pattern can be found in most sentences. Can you identify the actor and the action in each of the following sentences?

The teacher laughed.
The crowd applauded.

The actor in a sentence is called the **subject.** The action word in a sentence is called the **verb.** Together, the subject and the verb form the core of the sentence. Notice that even if extra words are added to the two sentences above, the subject–verb core in each sentence remains the same.

The teacher laughed at the student's joke.
After the performance, the crowd applauded enthusiastically.

You can see that to identify subjects and verbs, you must be able to separate these core words from the rest of the words in the sentence.
Here are some suggestions to help you identify verbs.

1. The *action* words in sentences are verbs. For example,

The team *played* well.
This store *sells* rare books.
The doctor *recommended* vitamins.

Underline the verb in each of the following sentences.

The bank lends money to small businesses.
Gina speaks Italian.
The flood destroyed many homes.

2. All forms of the verb "to be" are verbs: *am, is, are, was, were,* and *been.* For example,

Susan *is* unhappy.
The actor *was* nervous.

Verbs also include words that can be used as substitutes for forms of *be,* such as *seem, feel, become,* and *appear.* These verbs are called **linking verbs.**

Susan *seems* unhappy.
The actor *appeared* nervous.

Underline the verb in each of the following sentences.

The children became excited during the birthday party.

The professor seemed fatigued today.

The actors felt happy with their performances.

3. Verbs are the only words that change their spelling to show tense. **Tense** is the time—present, past, or future—at which the verb's action occurs. For example, the sentence "We *walk* each morning" has a present-tense verb. The sentence "We *walked* each morning" has a past-tense verb. Underline the verb in each of the following sentences.

Grandfather moves today.

My brother moved to Chicago last month.

Sandra dances very well.

Maria danced on her wedding day.

I wash my hair every morning.

The nurse washed her hands.

Identifying verbs will be easier for you if you remember that the following kinds of words are *not* verbs.

4. An **infinitive**—the combination of the word *to* plus a verb, such as *to walk* or *to study*—is not considered part of the verb in a sentence. Read the following sentences.

He plans to swim later.

She wants to enter graduate school.

The main verbs in these two sentences are *plans* and *wants*. The infinitives *to swim* and *to enter* are not included. Underline the main verb in each of the following sentences.

Benjy decided to play his new video games.

The conductor promised to check our luggage.

5. **Adverbs**—words that describe a verb—are *not* part of the verb. Many commonly used adverbs end in *-ly*. The adverbs in the following sentences are italicized. Underline the verb in each sentence.

The guitarist played *badly.*

Phillipe rushed *quickly* to our rescue.

The mother *patiently* helped her children.

The words *not, never,* and *very* are also adverbs. Like other adverbs, these words are not part of the verb. Underline the verb in each of the following sentences. Do *not* include adverbs.

The dancers are not here yet.

He never studies for his tests.

The director spoke very carefully.

He is not a good mechanic.

José never remembers to close the door.

Now that you can identify verbs, here are some suggestions to help you identify subjects.

1. The subject of a sentence is most often a noun. A **noun** is the name of a person, place, or thing, such as *Julia, Houston,* or *pens.* A noun may also be the name of an abstract idea, such as *sadness* or *failure.* Underline the subject in each of the following sentences *once* and the verb *twice.* Remember that the verb is the *action,* and the subject is the *actor.*

   Kevin reads many books each month.

   The store closes at midnight.

   Athens hosted the 2004 Summer Olympics.

   Love conquers all.

2. The subject of a sentence may also be a **subject pronoun.** A **pronoun** is a word used in place of a noun, such as *she* (= *Julia*), *it* (= *Houston*), or *they* (= *pens*). The following words are subject pronouns:

   I, you, he, she, it, we, they

   Underline the subject in each of the following sentences *once* and the verb *twice.*

   He was elected president of the United States.

   Each spring they travel to Yosemite National Park.

   I always drink strong coffee.

We rarely have dinner out on weekdays.

You washed the dishes last night.

3. The subject of a sentence may also be a **gerund**. A **gerund** is an *-ing* form of a verb used as a noun. For example, in the sentence "Swimming is an excellent form of exercise," the subject of the sentence is the gerund *swimming*. Underline the gerund subjects in the following sentences *once* and the verbs *twice*.

Listening is difficult for young children.

Dieting makes me very hungry.

4. In **commands** (also known as **imperatives**), such as "Wash the dishes!", the subject is understood to be the subject pronoun *you* even though the word *you* is almost never included in the command. *You* is understood to be the subject of the following sentences:

Do your homework early.

Consider the alternative.

Underline the subject in each of the following sentences *once* and the verb *twice*. If the sentence is a command, write the subject *you* in parentheses at the beginning of the sentence.

Remember to wipe your feet before entering.

The judge reviewed the verdict.

They bowl every Wednesday.

Discuss these issues with your colleagues.

Identifying subjects will be easier for you if you remember that the following kinds of words are *not* subjects.

5. **Adjectives**—words that describe a noun—are *not* part of the subject. For example, in the sentence "The tall boy runs well," the subject is "boy," *not* "tall boy." In the sentence "A new car is a great joy," the subject is "car," *not* "new car." Underline the subject in each of the following sentences *once* and the verb *twice*.

A talented singer performed that song.

Chocolate cake is his favorite food.

Small pets delight our family.

An angry, bitter debate ended the program.

6. Words that show **possession,** or ownership, are *not* part of the subject. Words that show possession include nouns ending in an apostrophe (') combined with *s,* such as *Dina's* or *cat's.* They also include **possessive pronouns,** words that replace nouns showing ownership, such as *hers* (= *Dina's*) or *its* (= *cat's*). Possessive pronouns include the following words:

my, your, his, hers, its, our, their

Because words that show possession are *not* part of the subject, in the sentence "My dog has fleas," the subject is "dog," *not* "my dog." In the sentence "Sarah's mother is a doctor," the subject is "mother," *not* "Sarah's mother." Underline the subject in each of the following sentences *once* and the verb *twice.*

His daughter became a doctor.

My brother works in another city.

This beach's beauty is startling.

Harry's car needs a new battery.

Here is a final suggestion to help you identify subjects and verbs accurately.

Try to identify the verb in a sentence before you try to identify the subject.

A sentence may have many nouns, any of which could be the subject, but it will usually have only one or two verbs. For example,

The director of the play shouted angry words to all the actors and staff.

There are five nouns in the above sentence (*director, play, words, actors, staff*), any of which might be the subject. However, there is only one verb—*shouted.* Once you have identified the verb as *shouted,* all you have to ask yourself is, "Who or what shouted?" The answer is *director,* which is the subject of the sentence.

Identify the subject and verb in the following sentence, remembering to look for the verb first.

In the winter, our family travels to the mountains for our vacation.

Remember these basic points:

1. The action being performed in a sentence is the **verb.**
2. The person or thing performing the action is the **subject.**
3. A sentence consists of an *actor* performing an *action,* or, in other words, a **subject** plus a **verb.**

Every sentence you write will have a subject and a verb, so you must be able to identify subjects and verbs to write correctly. Therefore, as you do the exercises in this unit, apply the rules you have learned in each lesson, and think about what you are doing. Do not make random guesses. Grammar is based on logic, not on luck.

Underline the subject in each of the following sentences *once* and the verb *twice.* Add the subject *you* in parentheses if the sentence is a command.

That man won the contest yesterday.

Success makes us happy.

The ancient horse slowly pulled the cart.

Wisdom is endless.

Consider the virtues of discipline.

My little sister's dance recital was lots of fun.

A quiet garden is my favorite place to read.

Your family's last vacation sounds very exciting.

Exercise 1A

Underline the subject of each sentence *once* and the verb *twice*. Each sentence has one subject and one verb. *Remember to look for the verb first* before you try to identify the subject.

1. Childhood <u>hunger</u> <u>is</u> a major problem in many parts of the world.

2. <u>Malnutrition</u> <u>kills</u> 6 million children each year – an average of one death every six seconds.

3. Now a new <u>product</u> <u>has</u> the potential to save the lives of many of these children.

4. This product's <u>name</u> <u>is</u> Plumpynut.

5. <u>Plumpynut</u> <u>contains</u> peanut butter, dry milk, sugar, and extra vitamins and minerals.

6. <u>Plumpynut</u> <u>is</u> very easy to use.

7. <u>It</u> <u>comes</u> in a small foil pouch.

8. To feed their children, <u>mothers</u> simply <u>squeeze</u> the Plumpynut paste into their children's mouths.

9. Malnourished <u>children</u> often <u>lose</u> interest in food.

10. However, <u>they</u> love <u>to eat</u> Plumpynut because of its sweet taste.

11. Another advantage of <u>Plumpynut</u> <u>is</u> its low price.

12. Feeding a child <u>Plumpynut</u> <u>costs</u> about one dollar per week.

13. Sick <u>children</u> quickly <u>recover</u> with Plumpynut.

14. Their average weight <u>gain</u> <u>is</u> two pounds per week.

15. Medical groups build Plumpynut distribution sites in needy areas.

16. Mothers come to these sites once a week to get Plumpynut for their children.

17. Medical personnel weigh the children each week.

18. They also monitor the children for infections and other diseases.

19. Some new patients appear near death from starvation.

20. These very ill children go to a hospital at the site.

21. They return home after only a few weeks' treatment with Plumpynut.

22. Their mothers continue to feed them Plumpynut at home.

23. Plumpynut is also easy to manufacture in small factories.

24. Some African and Caribbean nations now produce Plumpynut for their own residents.

25. Small factories throughout a nation provide a steady supply of Plumpynut for needy children.

26. They also give jobs to a community's parents.

Exercise 1B

Underline the subject of each sentence *once* and the verb *twice*. Each sentence has one subject and one verb. *Remember to look for the verb first* before you try to locate the subject.

1. Many Americans come from other countries.

2. My parents, for example, lived in Russia for many years.

3. They came to America to begin a new life.

4. American culture was different from their original culture.

5. Becoming American was their desire.

6. However, they had a difficult time at the beginning.

7. One difficulty was their language problem.

8. They spoke English poorly.

9. They often felt awkward and self-conscious.

10. Some salespeople at the grocery store even laughed at their English pronunciation.

11. These experiences hurt my parents' feelings.

12. My mother's reaction was to stay home as much as possible.

13. Then my parents decided to attend school to learn English.

14. After a long day at their jobs, they attended evening English classes for immigrants.

15. Learning English made them very happy and proud.

16. In fact, my mother decided to continue her studies to complete her bachelor's degree.

17. She studied each evening after dinner.

18. My father was very proud of my mother's discipline and dedication to her studies.

19. Receiving her bachelor's degree motivated my mother to continue to study for her teaching credential.

20. Today, she teaches English in Los Angeles, California, to high school students from many different countries.

CHAPTER 2

MULTIPLE SUBJECTS AND VERBS

Some sentences have more than one subject. Others have more than one verb. Many sentences have more than one subject *and* more than one verb. The subjects in the following sentences have been labeled with an "S" and the verbs with a "V."

```
 S    V      V
He swam and fished this summer.
```

```
      S      S     V
The dog and kitten became good friends.
```

```
 S     V              S       V
She danced well, and the director applauded.
```

```
      S     V      S        V
When we study hard, we usually do well.
```

You can identify the pattern of a sentence by indicating how many subjects and verbs it has. In theory, a sentence can have any number of subjects and verbs, but these are the most common patterns:

S–V	one subject and one verb
S–V–V	one subject and two verbs
S–S–V	two subjects and one verb
S–V/S–V	two subjects and two verbs

Underline the subjects of the following sentences *once* and the verbs *twice*.

The parrot squawked loudly.

His job started early and ended quite late.

Gardening and decorating were Beatrice's joys.

The team won the game, but the captain was not happy.

Any group of words that *contains at least one subject and one verb* is called a clause. A single sentence may have one clause or more than one clause.

S–V	one clause	The boy ate his pizza slice.
S–V–V	one clause	Sonya danced and sang.
S–S–V	one clause	The judge and the attorneys conferred.
S–V/S–V	two clauses	The dog barked, / and we laughed.
S–V–V/S–V	two clauses	He hiked and fished / when the sun rose.

Later in this book we will study the different types of clauses to understand how they determine punctuation. For now, the important thing is to learn to find all the subjects and verbs in each sentence.

Something to keep in mind when looking for multiple subjects and verbs is that the *length* of the sentence won't necessarily tell you whether the sentence has one clause or several clauses. Look at these two sentences:

She sang, but I danced. (How many clauses?)

The anxious, nervous young bride tripped on the stairs. (How many clauses?)

The first sentence is short—only five words—but it has two S–V patterns and, therefore, two clauses (*she sang*, but *I danced*). The second sentence is more than twice as long as the first, but it has only one clause (*bride . . . tripped*). So don't be fooled by the length of the sentence: Some short sentences have multiple subjects and verbs, and some long sentences have only a single clause (S–V).

The sentences below are skeleton sentences. That is, they are stripped down to only subjects, verbs, and connecting words. Go through them, underlining the subjects *once* and the verbs *twice*.

[Sarah laughed and joked.] S

Julia and Ben argued and fought.

The poet, the artist, and the teacher spoke.

After the game ended, we had lunch.

Laughter invigorates, and love binds.

Because it snowed, we stayed home.

When the movie ended, we left.

The philosopher and his ideas were exciting.

As we watched and waited, the river flooded.

If you go, I stay.

Janice wrote and revised.

As we listened, the storyteller entranced us.

He cried while she packed.

Watch your spelling! (Did you remember to put *You* in front?)

The practice sentences below have multiple subjects and verbs, but they also include the other types of words you studied in Chapter 1. Before you try them, review that chapter quickly to remind yourself about **adverbs** and **infinitives,** which are never part of the verb, and about **adjectives** and **possessives,** which are not part of the subject. Underline verbs *twice* and subjects *once*.

My uncles and aunts contribute to our family.

The long road seemed to run on for miles and miles.

Duane, José, and Clarence always loved to play soccer.

The gymnastic tournament finally ended, and the players went home.

After the spring semester ended, we partied a lot.

The terribly boring professor lectured monotonously to his class of students.

The boy's mother and father decided to send him to space camp.

The jury's verdict gladdened and relieved us.

The story's ending surprised us, but we still liked it.

Our new, fancy, expensive car has a CD player and a sun roof.

Keep off the grass, and don't pick the flowers!

✴ Exercise 2A

Underline the subjects of the following sentences *once* and the verbs *twice*. Remember not to include infinitives as part of the verb. To help you, the pattern of each sentence is indicated in parentheses.

1. This story is an old Korean folktale. (S–V)

2. It seems especially humorous to Koreans because in the past Korean women supposedly obeyed their husbands. (S–V/S–V)

3. A small town in Korea once had a very good mayor. (S–V)

4. The mayor did his job well, and everyone respected him. (S–V/S–V)

5. Unfortunately, this good man had one serious problem. (S–V)

6. He was a henpecked husband. (S–V)

7. His wife constantly nagged and scolded him. (S–V–V)

8. Whenever he was at home, he never had a moment's peace. (S–V/S–V)

9. One day the mayor decided to find a solution for his problem. (S–V)

10. He called a meeting of all the married men in his town. (S–V)

11. The men came to the town hall and seated themselves inside. (S–V–V)

12. First, the mayor separated the henpecked husbands from the rest of the men. (S–V)

13. He told the henpecked husbands to move to the right side of the room while the other men went to the left side. (S–V/S–V)

14. Ninety-nine men moved to the right side of the room, and only one man moved to the left. (S–V/S–V)

15. The mayor and the ninety-nine other henpecked husbands stared at the one man on the left side of the room. (S–S–V)

16. If he really had a peaceful home life, they wanted to learn his secret. (S–V/S–V)

17. The man seemed nervous, but he finally spoke. (S–V/S–V)

18. "I know nothing about the purpose of this meeting because I came in late." (S–V/S–V)

19. "I sat on the left side of the room only because my wife always tells me to stay away from crowds." (S–V/S–V)

✶ EXERCISE 2B

Underline the subjects of the following sentences *once* and the verbs *twice*. Some sentences may have more than one subject, more than one verb, or both.

1. We all want a happy life, but happiness is tricky to achieve.

2. Many books discuss the topic of happiness and analyze its meaning.

3. For some writers, happiness lies deep within us, and we need to examine ourselves to discover it.

4. These books and articles suggest activities like yoga and meditation to help us find inner happiness.

5. If happiness comes from something inside of us, we need to "work on ourselves" to become happy.

6. In contrast, some social scientists provide a different explanation for personal happiness.

7. In their opinion, external factors cause us to be happy.

8. These factors include our living conditions and our social interactions.

9. Researchers measure happiness levels for different countries.

10. Psychologists at the University of Leicester in Britain created the world's first map of happiness.

11. Some nations are better at producing happy people than others.

12. For example, the people of Denmark are very happy, but the citizens of Moldavia tend to be gloomy.

13. Although countries in Latin America are not rich, they are among the happiest places in the world.

14. The key to their happiness lies in their close family ties.

15. Strong family relationships support people in times of trouble and give them opportunities to enjoy being together in happy times.

16. People vary tremendously from country to country in relating to one another.

17. It is difficult for some Americans to maintain close family ties because Americans often move away from their hometowns.

18. Each year, about 40 million Americans move to a new city or state.

19. They hope to become happier by changing external factors in their lives, like their homes and their jobs.

20. To some psychologists, putting too much emphasis on being happy is self-defeating.

21. To these experts, happiness comes naturally if people live productive lives.

22. They compare life to a journey and think of happiness as a by-product of everyday experiences.

23. They often quote a familiar proverb.

24. "Happiness is not a destination but a manner of traveling."

C H A P T E R

3

DISTINGUISHING BETWEEN OBJECTS OF PREPOSITIONS AND SUBJECTS

ne of the most common causes of errors in identifying the subject of a sentence is confusing it with a noun used as the object of a preposition. This kind of error can also lead to mistakes in subject–verb agreement. (Subject–verb agreement is covered in Unit 2 of this book.) To avoid making this type of mistake, you first must learn to recognize prepositions and prepositional phrases.

Prepositions are the short words in our language that show the *position* or relationship between one word and another. For example, if you were trying to describe where a particular store was located, you might say:

The store is *on* the right.

The store is *near* the highway.

The store is *by* the bank.

The store is *under* the elm tree.

The store is *behind* the garage.

The italicized words are all prepositions. They indicate the position of the store in relation to the right, the freeway, the bank, the elm tree, and the garage.

Here is a list of the most common prepositions. You do not have to memorize these words, but you must be able to recognize them as prepositions when you see them.

about	between	of
above	beyond	on
across	by	onto
after	concerning	out
against	down	over
along	during	through
amid	except	to
among	for	toward
around	from	under
at	in	up
before	inside	upon
behind	into	with
below	like	within
beneath	near	without
beside		

As you can see from the example sentences describing the location of the store, prepositions are not used by themselves; they are always placed in front of a noun or a pronoun. The noun or pronoun following the preposition is called the **object of the preposition.** The group of words containing the preposition and its object is called a **prepositional phrase.** Any words, such as adjectives or the words *a, an,* or *the,* that come between the preposition and its object are also part of the prepositional phrase. Read the following sentences, in which the prepositional phrases are italicized. Notice that each prepositional phrase begins with a preposition and ends with a noun or a pronoun.

I leaned *against the car.*

He walked *toward the nearest exit.*

The glass *of orange juice* costs fifty cents.

She stood *beside me.*

Some prepositional phrases may have more than one object.

You may sit *near Jane or Susan.*

You may have some *of the bread or waffles.*

It is also possible to have two or more prepositional phrases in a row.

We looked *for the clues in the forest.*

The director *of that movie at the local theater* is sitting by us.

Circle the prepositional phrases in the following sentences. Some sentences may have more than one prepositional phrase.

The policeman looked carefully around the room.

The keys to the car are in the glove compartment.

I gave your recipe to my next-door neighbor.

Ruth came to the party with me.

Construct sentences of your own containing prepositional phrases. Use the prepositions listed below. Make certain that each of your sentences contains at least one subject and one verb.

with: _____

through: _____

by: _____

of: _____

at: _____

The words *before* and *after* may be used either as prepositions or as conjunctions (see below). If the word is being used as a preposition, it will be followed by a noun or pronoun object. If the word is being used as a conjunction, it will be followed by both a subject and a verb.

As a Preposition	*As a Conjunction*
I go to bed *before midnight*.	*Before* you leave the house, be sure to lock the door.
Bob entered the room *after me*.	*After* the bell rang, the students left the room.

What do prepositional phrases have to do with identifying subjects and verbs? The answer is simple.

Any word that is part of a prepositional phrase cannot be the subject or the verb of a sentence.

This rule works for two reasons:

1. Any noun or pronoun in a prepositional phrase must be the object of the preposition, and the object of a preposition cannot also be a subject.
2. Prepositional phrases never contain verbs.

To see how this rule can help you identify subjects and verbs, read the following seventeen-word sentence:

At the height of the rush hour, my car stalled in the middle of a busy intersection.

If you want to find the subject and the verb of this sentence, you know that they will not be part of any of the sentence's prepositional phrases. So, cross out all the prepositional phrases in the sentence.

~~At the height of the rush hour,~~ my car stalled ~~in the middle of a busy intersection.~~

You now have only three words left out of the original seventeen, and you know that the subject and the verb must be within these three words. What are the subject and the verb?

Read the following sentence, and cross out all of its prepositional phrases.

In the evening she works on her assignments for the next day.

If you crossed out all the prepositional phrases, you should be left with only two words—the subject *she* and the verb *works*.

Identify the subject and the verb in the following sentence. Cross out the prepositional phrases first.

On the way to their hotel, a group of tourists stopped at a souvenir shop.

If you have identified all of the prepositional phrases, you should be left with only three words—*a group* and *stopped.* Which word is the subject, and which is the verb?

Now you can see another reason why it is important to be able to identify prepositional phrases. It might seem logical for the subject of the sentence to be *tourists.* However, because *of tourists* is a prepositional phrase, *tourists* cannot be the subject. Instead, the subject is *group.*

What is the subject of the following sentence?

Many members of Congress are lawyers.

If you crossed out the prepositional phrase *of Congress,* you would know that the subject is *members,* not *Congress.*

Underline the subjects of the following sentences *once* and the verbs *twice.* Remember to cross out the prepositional phrases first.

~~During the oil shortage,~~ the price ~~of gas~~ increased.

The car ~~with the dented fender~~ belongs ~~to Carolyn.~~

A house ~~in Beverly Hills with three bedrooms and two bathrooms~~ sells ~~for more than $800,000.~~

The stores ~~in the mall~~ open, ~~at ten.~~ ~~in the morning.~~

The driver ~~of the red Corvette~~ skidded ~~into the center lane.~~

One ~~of the employees~~ received a $50 raise.

Your clothes ~~from the dry cleaner~~ are ~~in the closet.~~

modifier

EXERCISE 3A

Underline the subjects of the following sentences *once* and the verbs *twice*. Some sentences may have more than one subject and/or more than one verb. *Remember to cross out the prepositional phrases first.*

1. A cave ~~in Altamira,~~ Spain, contains some ~~of the world's finest Paleolithic (Old Stone Age) paintings.~~

2. The twelve-year-old daughter ~~of a Spanish archaeologist~~ discovered these paintings ~~by accident in 1879.~~

3. The girl's name was Maria Sautuola.

4. While her father searched the floor ~~of the cave for animal bones and stone tools,~~ Maria wandered ~~to another part of the cave.~~

5. ~~In this part of the cave,~~ she noticed pictures ~~of many different kinds of animals.~~

6. Maria was the first person ~~to see these paintings in more than 15,000 years.~~

7. Altamira became the first ~~of many discoveries of prehistoric cave paintings in Spain and France.~~

8. Drawings ~~of bison, boars, and deer in red, brown, black, and yellow pigments~~ cover the walls ~~and ceiling of the cave.~~

9. The handprints ~~of the artists~~ also appear ~~on the walls.~~

10. ~~In some places,~~ the artists painted ~~over curves and projections in the cave wall.~~

11. The shape ~~of the animals~~ follows the contours ~~of the stone.~~

12. Using this technique gives the animals ~~an amazingly three-dimensional, lifelike quality.~~

13. Historians sometimes call Altamira "the Sistine Chapel of the Ice Age" because ~~of the beauty of its art.~~

14. Unfortunately, the Spanish government had ~~to close the Altamira cave to the general public~~ in the 1970s.

15. Warmth ~~from the bodies of thousands of visitors, along with the heat from~~ electric lamps, allowed a fungus ~~to grow in the cave~~.

16. This fungus threatened ~~to destroy the paintings~~.

17. ~~Of course,~~ visitors still wanted ~~to see the Altamira paintings~~.

18. The government's solution was ~~to build a replica of the cave and its paintings near the original ca~~ve.

19. This replica allows visitors ~~to appreciate the artistry of the ancient paint~~ers ~~without damage to the original~~ art.

20. If you have ~~a chance to travel in Spain,~~ try ~~to include a visit to Altamira~~.

EXERCISE 3B

Underline the subject of each sentence *once* and the verb *twice*. Some sentences may have more than one subject, more than one verb, or both. Remember to cross out prepositional phrases first.

1. One of the most important inventions of all time is the computer.

2. The story of modern computers begins during the 1930s and spans many decades and countries.

3. In 1937, John Atanasoff and Clifford Berry designed the first electronic digital computer.

4. During World War II, a computer helped the Allies to win the war.

5. The name of the computer was the Colossus, and British intelligence agents used it to decipher German codes.

6. In 1946, two American scientists completed work on the first large-scale general-purpose digital computer.

7. With its 18,000 vacuum tubes, this computer used an enormous amount of electricity.

8. When scientists first turned the computer on in Philadelphia, the lights dimmed in an entire section of the city.

9. The history of the computer is really the story of gradual increases in technology.

10. The invention of the transistor in 1947 enabled later computers to use less electrical energy.

11. The American public's awareness of computers increased during the presidential election of 1950.

12. ~~To the amazement of everyone~~, the new UNIVAC <u>computer</u> correctly <u>predicted</u>
    Eisenhower's *obj* victory ~~after analyzing only 5 percent of the popular vote~~.

13. ~~In 1958~~, the invention of the integrated <u>circuit</u> <u>laid</u> the foundation ~~for high-
    speed computers~~ ~~with large-capacity memories~~.

14. Until the 1980s, <u>people</u> <u>used</u> computers mainly ~~in offices and factories~~.

15. Then, ~~in 1981~~, <u>IBM</u> <u>marketed</u> its first "personal *obj* computer," ~~or PC~~.

16. ~~The introduction of the new~~ <u>PCs</u> <u>made</u> *obj* computers available ~~for everyone~~.

17. Later ~~in the 1980s~~, the genius of <u>Steve Jobs</u> and <u>Steve Wozniak</u> <u>placed</u> Apple
    computers *obj* ~~in schools~~ ~~and colleges all over the country~~.

18. The <u>presence</u> ~~of computers in classrooms~~ <u>created</u> a whole new generation ~~of
    computer users~~.

19. ~~In 1982~~, ~~instead of *Time*~~ magazine's usual ~~"person of the year,"~~ the <u>computer</u>
    <u>became</u> the "Machine of the Year."

20. ~~In the later 1980~~s, the <u>introduction</u> ~~of laptop computers~~ <u>made</u> it possible ~~for
    people to use their computers anywhere~~.

21. ~~Even the writing~~ ~~of *Basic Grammar and Usage*~~ reflects the influence ~~of the
    computer~~.

22. The <u>authors</u> <u>wrote</u> *obj* early editions ~~of the book~~ ~~on electric typewriters and~~ cut
    and <u>pasted</u> sections ~~of the manuscript together~~.

23. When <u>they</u> <u>finished</u> the manuscript, <u>they</u> <u>mailed</u> all the typed pages ~~to their
    publisher~~.

24. Now the <u>authors</u> <u>use</u> their laptop computers ~~to write their book~~, and they
    send their manuscript ~~to the publisher on a CD~~.

CHAPTER 4

MAIN VERBS AND HELPING VERBS

Verbs can be either **main verbs** or **helping** (also called **auxiliary**) **verbs.** Main verbs are the kind of verb you have already studied. Main verbs tell what action is being performed in a sentence. For example,

I *drive* to work each day.

This restaurant *serves* Mexican food.

Helping verbs are used in combination with main verbs. They perform two major functions:

1. Helping verbs indicate shades of meaning that cannot be expressed by a main verb alone. Consider the differences in meaning in the following sentences, in which the helping verbs have been italicized.

I *may* marry you soon.   I *must* marry you soon.

I *should* marry you soon.   I *can* marry you soon.

As you can see, changing the helping verb changes the meaning of the entire sentence. These differences in meaning could not be expressed simply by using the main verb, *marry*, alone.

2. Helping verbs also show tense—the time at which the action of the verb takes place. Notice how changing the helping verb in the following sentences helps change the tense of the main verb *visit*. (Both the helping verbs and the main verbs have been italicized.)

He *is visiting* New York.

He *will visit* New York.

He *has visited* New York.

Notice the position that helping verbs have in a sentence. They always *come before* the main verb, although sometimes another word, such as an adverb, may come between the helping verb and the main verb.

The team *can win* the game.

The team *can* probably *win* the game.

You *should stay* in bed today.

You *should* definitely *stay* in bed today.

If a question contains a helping verb, the helping verb still *comes before* the main verb.

Can the team *win* the game?

Should you *stay* in bed today?

Does the car *run* well?

When *is* the plane *departing?*

The following words are helping verbs. Memorize them.

can, could

may, might, must

shall, should

will, would

The following words can be used either as helping verbs or as main verbs. They are helping verbs if they are used in combination with a main verb. They are main verbs if they occur alone. Memorize them.

has, have, had (forms of the verb *have*)

does, do, did, done (forms of the verb *do*)

am, is, are, was, were, been (forms of the verb *be*)

As Main Verbs	*As Helping Verbs*
He *has* my book.	He *has gone* home.
She *did* a headstand.	She *did* not *arrive* on time.
We *are* hungry.	We *are eating* soon.

From now on, whenever you are asked to identify the verbs in a sentence, *include all the main verbs and all the helping verbs*. For example, in the sentence "We should review this lesson," the complete verb is "should review." In the sentence "He has lost his wallet," the verb is "has lost." Underline the complete verbs in the following sentences.

Gail must borrow some money.

I may go to Hawaii this summer.

Sheila can speak German fluently.

We are leaving soon.

Some sentences may contain more than one helping verb.

one helping verb	The mechanic *is working* on your car.
two helping verbs	He *must have lost* your phone number.
three helping verbs	That bill *should have been paid* by now.

Underline the subjects of the following sentences *once* and the complete verbs *twice*.

You could have sold your car for a better price.

The weather will be getting warmer soon.

You have not been listening to me.

Do you have a part-time job?

You should have gone to the dentist last week.

My cousin may be visiting me this summer.

Remember this rule:

The verbs in a sentence include all the main verbs plus all the helping verbs.

Exercise 4A

Underline the subjects of the following sentences *once* and the complete verbs *twice*. Some sentences may have more than one subject, more than one verb, or both. Remember to cross out prepositional phrases first.

1. People need salt ~~in order to live~~, so salt has always played an important role ~~in human history~~.

2. Early humans hunted animals for food, and the meat from these animals provided them with enough salt.

3. After people began to grow crops for food and to eat less meat, they needed to find other sources of salt.

4. Salt can be extracted ~~from sea water or salty springs by evaporation~~, or it can be mined ~~from the earth~~.

5. Until modern times, salt was often scarce, and it became a very valuable product.

6. In ancient times, salt was sometimes used as money.

7. The Greeks could purchase slaves with salt.

8. A weak or undesirable slave was described as "not worth his salt," and we still hear this expression today.

9. The soldiers of the Roman legions received part of their wages in salt.

10. This salt payment was called a *salarium* ~~in Latin~~, and it is the source ~~of our English word~~ *salary*.

11. Because salt was such an important product, governments often taxed it in order to raise funds.

12. Ancient Chinese emperors levied taxes on salt, and the British government collected salt taxes in both colonial America and in colonial India.

13. In 1930, Mahatma Gandhi led people in India on a two-hundred-mile march to the sea to collect tax-free salt for the poor and to protest British rule.

14. In eighteenth-century France, kings sold the right to produce salt to only a few wealthy men, and salt became very scarce and expensive.

15. This scarcity of salt was one of the causes of the French Revolution.

16. As in twentieth-century India, the high price of salt became a symbol of the government's oppression of the poor.

17. Before modern times, salt was used to preserve food.

18. People learned to enjoy the salty taste of food like ham, and cheese, and olives.

19. Fine restaurants and gourmet stores now offer specialty salts, like pink river salt from Australia or black ocean salt from Hawaii.

20. However, some people must limit their salt intake in order to control their blood pressure.

21. For these people, markets sell many low-salt items, from soup to potato chips to alcoholic beverages.

22. Even if we need to limit our consumption of salt, it continues to play an important role in our diets.

EXERCISE 4B

Underline the subjects of the following sentences *once* and the verbs *twice*. Some sentences may have more than one subject, more than one set of verbs, or both. Remember to cross out the prepositional phrases first.

1. Sometimes seemingly ordinary people may do extraordinarily brave things.

2. The courage of these people can serve as an inspiration to all of us.

3. In southern France, during World War II, the inhabitants of a small rural village risked their own lives to save five thousand Jewish men, women, and children.

4. Located in the mountains of south-central France, Le Chambon-sur-Lignon had been a farming village for centuries.

5. ~~During World War II~~, the French Vichy government collaborated ~~with the Nazis~~ and participated ~~in the roundup and extermination of France's Jewish population.~~ *english*

6. When the French government surrendered to the Nazis, the village pastor reminded his congregation to resist the Vichy government and the Nazis by using "weapons of the spirit."

7. The villagers responded by beginning their program of hiding Jews from the Nazis.

8. Anyone in danger was given shelter by these remarkable people, and nobody was turned away.

9. For example, some villagers owned businesses and hired Jews to work for them.

10. Other Jewish refugees were hidden ~~in the villagers' homes~~ or ~~on their farms~~.

11. Entire families were involved in rescuing the Jews, and even children helped to hide them.

12. An elaborate system of signals was used to warn the Jewish refugees if danger was near.

13. In the years after World War Two, the villagers of Le Chambon would become known around the world for their courage and would be the subject of books and films.

14. If the rescuers had been caught by the Nazis, they would have faced arrest, torture, and execution.

15. Why would people risk their own lives and the lives of their children to save the lives of strangers?

16. Because he had survived the war as a baby in Le Chambon, Pierre Sauvage tried to answer these questions in his film *Weapons of the Spirit*.

17. Even a few Vichy officials may have known about the villagers and the Jews during the war but said and did nothing.

18. Perhaps they too were impressed by the courage of the villagers.

19. Pierre Sauvage uses the term "conspiracy of kindness" to explain the unusual actions of these officials.

20. If the villagers are asked to explain their actions, they will only smile and shrug their shoulders.

21. In their opinion, their actions should be considered completely normal.

22. The villagers of Le Chambon have provided all of us with a very positive example of "normal" behavior!

UNIT 1 REVIEW

Underline the subjects of the following sentences *once* and the complete verbs, including all helping verbs, *twice*. Remember to cross out prepositional phrases first.

1. Has anyone offered you "a penny ~~for your thoughts~~" recently?

2. Pennies may soon disappear if some economists have their way.

3. ~~In the opinion of these experts~~, the penny has outlived its usefulness.

4. Almost nothing can be bought now ~~for less than a nickel~~.

5. The penny's main function is to make change, not to purchase individual items.

6. In addition, it now costs more than one cent ~~to make each penny~~.

7. Pennies were formerly made ~~of copper~~.

8. Because copper has become a very expensive metal, today's pennies are made of zinc, with only a thin copper coating ~~on the outside~~.

9. However, even a mostly zinc penny costs almost two cents to produce.

10. Using pennies can also waste a lot of time.

11. Jeff Gore is the head of the group Citizens for Retiring the Penny.

12. According to Gore's calculations, handling pennies adds two and a half seconds to a financial transaction.

13. The average American must spend four extra hours each year just to handle pennies.

14. Many pennies are not circulated but are stored in people's homes in jars or piggy banks.

CHAPTER 5

RECOGNIZING SINGULAR AND PLURAL SUBJECTS AND VERBS

Errors in **subject–verb** agreement are among the most common grammatical mistakes. By applying the rules in this unit, you should be able to correct many of the errors in your own writing. As you already know, a sentence must contain both a subject and a verb. Read the following two sentences. What is the grammatical difference between them?

The bank opens at ten o'clock in the morning.

The banks open at ten o'clock in the morning.

In the first sentence, the subject *bank* is singular. **Singular** means "one." There is one bank in the first sentence. In the second sentence, the subject *banks* is plural. **Plural** means "two or more." There are at least two (and possibly more than two) banks in the second sentence.

Like the subject *bank*, the verb *opens* in the first sentence is singular. Verb forms ending in *-s* are used with *singular* subjects, as in the sentence "The bank

45

opens at ten o'clock in the morning." The verb *open* in the second sentence above is plural. This verb form (without a final *-s*) is used with *plural* subjects, as in the sentence "The banks *open* at ten o'clock in the morning."

In other words, if the subject of a sentence is *singular,* the verb in the sentence must also be *singular.* If the subject of the sentence is *plural,* the verb must be *plural.* This matching of singular subjects with singular verbs and plural subjects with plural verbs is called **subject–verb agreement.**

To avoid making mistakes in subject–verb agreement, you must be able to recognize the difference between singular and plural subjects and verbs.

The subjects of sentences are usually nouns or pronouns. As you know, the plurals of nouns are usually formed by adding an *-s* to singular forms.

Singular	*Plural*
envelope	envelopes
restaurant	restaurants

However, a few nouns (under 1 percent) have irregular plural forms.

Singular	*Plural*
man	men
leaf	leaves
child	children
thesis	theses
self	selves
medium	media (as in the "mass media")

Pronouns that can be used as subjects are also singular or plural, depending on whether they refer to one or more than one person, place, or thing.

Singular	*Plural*
I	we
you	you
he, she, it	they

Notice that the pronoun *you* may be either singular or plural.

If nouns show number by adding *-s* to the plural, what do verbs do to show whether a verb is singular or plural? A long time ago, English verbs had many different endings for this purpose, but most of those endings have been dropped. Today most English verbs look the same whether the subject is singular or plural: "I talk," "we talk," "the men talk," "I remembered," "they remembered," "the class remembered," and so on. However, there is one place where English verbs have kept a special ending to show number. That special ending is also an *-s,* and the place where it is added is in the present-tense singular with the subject pronouns *he, she, it* and with any singular noun that could replace any of these pronouns. Look at these sentences written in the present tense, and notice when the *-s* is added to the verb:

Singular	*Plural*
I talk.	We talk.
You talk.	You talk.
He talks.	They talk.
She talks.	They talk.
It talks.	They talk.
The man talks.	The men talk.
The girl talks.	The girls talk.

To sum up, although adding an *-s* to most nouns (99 percent) makes them plural, some singular verbs also end with an *-s.* An easy way to remember this difference is to memorize this rule:

Any verb ending in *-s* is singular.

There are no exceptions to this rule. Therefore, it is not good usage in college writing to have a sentence in which a plural subject is matched with a verb ending in *-s.*

Effective writers are as aware of **usage** as they are of grammar. Good usage means choosing different kinds of language for different situations, just as we choose different clothes for different occasions. In **informal** situations, such as conversations with friends, it is common to choose informal usage. However, almost all of the writing you do for college is in **formal** situations, such as exams and essay assignments. The difference between formal and informal usage can be seen when we make subjects agree with their verbs. Because most conversation is very informal, you may have heard or have used many informal verb choices in your own conversations. Notice the differences in usage in these examples:

Informal	*Formal*
We was here.	We were here.
He don't come here.	He doesn't come here.
They was at the beach.	They were at the beach.

You want your college writing to be as effective as you can make it. In college you must choose **formal usage** in almost every situation—essays, reports, exams, and so on. The exercises in this book are *always* designed for you to choose formal usage.

To avoid subject–verb agreement errors, there are some rules that you should keep in mind. (How you "keep rules in mind" is up to you. If you find that even after you study rules, you still cannot remember them, you should *memorize* the rules in this unit.)

Rule 1. A verb agrees with the subject, not with the complement. A **complement** is a word that refers to the same person or thing as the subject of the sentence. It follows a linking verb.

S   LV   C

Our main economic *problem is* rising prices.

In the sentence above, the subject is *problem,* which is singular. The subject is not *prices.* Rather, *prices* is the complement. Therefore, the linking verb takes the singular form *is* to agree with *problem.* If the sentence is reversed, it reads:

S   LV   C

Rising *prices are* our main economic problem.

The subject is now the plural noun *prices,* and *problem* is the complement. The verb now takes the plural form *are.* Which are the correct verbs in the following sentences?

The topic of discussion (was, were) political refugees.

Astrological signs (seems, seem) to be an interesting subject to many people.

Rule 2. Prepositional phrases have no effect on a verb.

The *president,* with his chief economic advisors, is having a press conference today.

In the sentence above, the subject is singular (*president*). The prepositional phrase, *with his chief economic advisors,* has no effect on the verb, which remains singular (*is having*).

A hamburger with French fries costs two dollars.

The singular verb *costs* agrees with the singular subject *hamburger.* The prepositional phrase *with French fries* has no effect on the verb. Which is the correct verb in the following sentence?

The woman with her ten cats (was, were) evicted for breaking the clause in her lease that prohibited the keeping of pets.

In addition, do not mistakenly make your verb agree with a noun or pronoun in a prepositional phrase. (This is easy to do because many prepositional phrases come just before a verb.)

The *problems* of this school district *trouble* the school board greatly.

In the sentence above, the subject is plural (*problems*). The plural verb *trouble* agrees with *problems*, not with the singular object of the preposition (*district*).

The attitude of adolescents is often difficult to understand.

The singular verb *is* agrees with the singular subject *attitude*, not with the plural object of the preposition (*adolescents*).

Which are the correct verbs in the following sentences?

One of the restaurants (serves, serve) Thai food.

The directions for the test (was, were) confusing.

Rule 3. Be especially alert for subject–verb agreement when the sentence has **inverted word order,** as in these three situations:

a) Questions

Notice the location of the subject in these questions:

HV S MV
Does he want a new car? (subject between helping and main verb)

V   S
Is turkey your favorite food? (subject after main verb)

Interrogative words like *when, where,* and *how* come at the beginning of sentence patterns, but they are never subjects.

HV   S MV
When *does* the *game start?* (subject between helping and main verb)

MV   S
Where *is* the *picnic?* (subject after verb)

HV S MV
How *can he study* all weekend? (subject between helping and main verb)

b)   **Sentence patterns beginning with *here* or *there***

The words *here* and *there* are never subjects.
Notice the location of the subject in these patterns:

There *are* many *children* here today. (subject after verb)

Here *are* your test *results*. (subject after verb)

c)   **Rare patterns in which the verb precedes the subject**

Occasionally a writer will, for emphasis, put a subject after its verb.
Notice the location of the subject in these sentences:

Behind the lamp in the corner *was* the very expensive *statue*. (If the order of
this sentence were reversed, it would read, "The very expensive statue was
behind the lamp in the corner.")

Toward the finish line *raced* the breathless *runner.* ("The breathless runner
raced toward the finish line.")

Exercise 5A

Circle the verb that correctly completes each sentence. Make certain that you have crossed out prepositional phrases and that you have identified the correct subject.

1. Each year Americans (spends, spend) more than $40 billion on their pets.

2. The sale of luxury items for pets (accounts, account) for part of this amount.

3. For example, one of the new trends in pet care (is, are) hotels for cats and dogs.

4. In the past, if a pet needed a temporary place to live, its usual accommodations (was, were) a kennel.

5. The services of a kennel (includes, include) a small metal cage for the pet to sleep in plus food and water and exercise once a day.

6. However, there (is, are) many more services available for the pampered pets in a pet hotel.

7. Instead of a small cage, the residents of a pet hotel (lives, live) in airy "atrium rooms."

8. Even more luxurious accommodations (is, are) provided in the hotel's suites.

9. The furnishings of a suite (includes, include) a raised dog bed and a television.

10. A hypoallergenic lambskin blanket (covers, cover) each bed.

11. Which programs (does, do) a pet hotel resident watch on its personal television set?

12. A popular choice (is, are) Walt Disney's *101 Dalmatians*.

13. Watching a movie sometimes (makes, make) a pet hungry.

14. The hotel's fat-free and lactose-free ice cream (provides, provide) a healthy snack.

15. With ordinary kennels, a pet owner (has, have) no way to stay in contact with his or her pet.

16. Along with the other amenities of a pet hotel suite (comes, come) access to a telephone.

17. Daily phone calls from its owner (helps, help) to keep a pet happy.

18. Recreation, along with food and lodging, (is, are) also provided for each hotel guest.

19. A variety of pet toys and exercise equipment (is, are) available in the hotel's large indoor playroom.

20. Supervision of the playroom by hotel employees (prevents, prevent) conflicts among the animals.

21. The services of a beauty salon (is, are) available to the pets so that they can look their best when their owners return.

22. A one-night stay in a pet hotel suite currently (costs, cost) about thirty-five dollars.

EXERCISE 5B

Some of the sentences in this exercise contain subject-verb agreement errors. Others are correct as written. If a sentence contains an agreement error, cross out the incorrect verb, and write the correct verb in its place. If a sentence has no agreement errors, label it C for *correct*.

1. One of the world's major problems are food shortages. *C*

2. With the rapid growth of the world's population ~~have come~~ *came* the need to produce food more quickly and efficiently.

3. A partial solution to this problem ~~are~~ *is* growing more potatoes.

4. The potato produces nutritious food faster and on less land than any other crop. *C*

5. The nutritional value of potatoes make them a staple food in many countries. *C*

6. A serving of potatoes ~~provide~~ *provides* large amounts of fiber, vitamin C, and potassium.

7. In addition, for people with limited dietary resources, the large amount of starch in potatoes satisfy the need for a filling, high-calorie food. *C*

8. One indication of the importance of potatoes ~~are~~ *is* the efforts of scientists to ensure the potato's future survival.

9. Most research on potatoes come from the International Potato Center in Lima, Peru. *C*

10. Why is the center for research on potatoes located in Lima? *C*

11. The Andes Mountains of Peru ~~was~~ *is* the original home of the potato.

12. The importance of potatoes to this region's people ~~are~~ *is* evident in their language.

13. In the vocabulary of the Quechua Indians of Peru is [*are*] more than one hundred names for potatoes.

14. More than five thousand varieties of potato is [*are*] stored at the International Potato Center.

15. This large selection of potatoes help to ensure genetic variation. *C*

16. Lack of genetic variation sometimes leads to the failure of a region's entire potato crop. *C*

17. For example, in nineteenth-century Ireland, only a few kinds of potatoes were grown. *C*

18. Between 1846 and 1848, almost the entire crop of Irish potatoes were killed by a single virus. *C*

19. The 1.5 million deaths from the Irish Potato Famine still rank as one of the worst natural disasters in European history. *C*

20. Keeping many varieties of potatoes alive help to protect the world from another such famine. *C*

21. In addition, different kinds of potatoes thrive in different parts of the world. *C*

22. Having access to a large variety of potatoes allow [*allows*] scientists to develop the best potatoes for particular climates and regions.

CHAPTER 6

INDEFINITE PRONOUNS AS SUBJECTS

The subject pronouns we have been studying, like *she* or *it* or *they*, refer to specific, definite persons, places, or things. This chapter is about another kind of pronoun, **indefinite pronouns**, which do not refer to a specific person or place or to definite things.

Rule 4. The following indefinite pronouns are **singular** and require **singular** verbs:

anybody, anyone, anything

each, each one

either, neither

everybody, everyone, everything

nobody, no one, nothing

somebody, someone, something

55

Everybody has his camping gear.

Anything goes.

Each of the players *knows* the ground rules.

Either of those times *is* all right with me.

Notice that in the last two sentences, the verbs agree with the singular subjects *each* and *either*. The verbs are not affected by the plural nouns in the prepositional phrases *of the players* or *of those times*.

Rule 5 Indefinite pronouns, such as the words *some, half, most,* and *all,* may take either singular or plural verbs, depending on their meaning in the context of the sentence. If these words tell **how much** of something is meant, the verb is singular; but if they tell **how many** of something is meant, the verb is plural.

Most of the bread *is* stale. (how much?)

Most of the actors *are* present. (how many?)

Some of the money *is* missing. (how much?)

Some of the players *were* late. (how many?)

All of the fortune *goes* to the family. (how much?)

All of these items *go* to us. (how many?)

Do not confuse the words in this rule with the words *each, either,* and *neither* in Rule 4. Those three words *always* require a singular verb.

how much – singular
how many – plural

EXERCISE 6A

Part 1: Circle the verb that correctly completes each sentence. This section of the exercise covers only rules from Chapter 6.

1. Everyone (**needs**, need) a passport to travel to foreign countries.

2. Neither of those jobs (**offers**, offer) good benefits.

3. Some of my classmates (plans, **plan**) to join the army after they graduate.

4. Most of these automobiles (has, **have**) front and side air bags.

5. (**Has**, have) anyone forgotten to sign the petition?

6. Each of the banks (**offers**, offer) free checking accounts to senior citizens.

7. Half of the college's classes (is, **are**) taught by teaching assistants.

8. Half of the money for the new highway (comes, **come**) from the federal government.

Part 2: Some of the sentences in Part 2 contain subject-verb agreement errors. Others are correct as written. If a sentence contains an agreement error, cross out the incorrect verb, and write the correct verb in its place. If a sentence has no agreement errors, label it *C* for *correct*. The sentences in Part 2 cover rules from both Chapters 5 and 6.

9. My favorite dessert ~~are~~ is chocolate chip cookies.

10. Each of the author's novels have a similar plot. C

11. Neither of those houses ~~has~~ have enough bedrooms for our family.

12. Hot weather with high humidity ~~make~~ made Washington, D.C., an uncomfortable place to live during the summer.

13. This agency's main concern ~~are~~ is neglected children.

14. The design, along with the quality of the weaving, determine the price of a handmade carpet. _C_

15. A crowd of people usually gather [gathered] at the scene of an accident.

16. Some of the cab drivers in New York City seem [seemed] to disregard the speed limits.

17. Included with each vacuum cleaner are a set of attachments for cleaning upholstery and dusting furniture. _C_

18. Most of the information in these reports has [have] to be updated.

19. A mother with two ill children are [were] waiting to see the doctor.

20. Among John's problems were [one is] a lack of money.

21. Half of Tom's stocks have lost money in the last six months. _C_

22. Most of the factory's equipment need to be replaced. _C_

23. Each of the jurors agree [agreed] that the defendant is guilty.

24. Here are [is] a collection of record albums from the 1960s.

25. The price of meals are not included in the tour package. _C_

how many = plural
how much = singular

EXERCISE 6B

Some of the sentences in this exercise contain subject-verb agreement errors. Others are correct as written. If a sentence contains an agreement error, cross out the incorrect verb, and write in the correct form. If a sentence has no agreement errors, label it *C* for *correct*. This exercise covers the rules from Chapters 5 and 6.

1. Everyone recognize*s* the remarkable sound of a wolf howling.

2. The long, lonely howl ~~of the wolf in the middle~~ of the night *is* ~~are~~ one of the more beautiful sounds in nature.

3. The future of wolves in the western United States have been a concern of environmentalists since the 1980s. *C*

4. Wolves frequently attack deer and elk, so most of the western wolf population ~~was~~ *were* nearly exterminated in some states.

5. Another enemy of the wolves ~~were~~ *(was)* ranchers because wolves also kill livestock.

6. From the mid-1990s through 2008, the number of wolves in the West increased under the protection of the Federal Endangered Species Act. *C*

7. Under this act, the killing of wolves ~~were~~ *was* prohibited in a number of western states.

8. ~~In addition, in 1995~~ a group ~~of sixty-six wolves~~ ~~were~~ *was* reintroduced ~~into Yellowstone National Park~~, after an absence there ~~of nearly seventy years~~. *C*

9. Some of the wolves in the pack ~~was~~ *were* given radio collars so that scientists could track them.

10. One of the other tactics used to track the wolves ~~were~~ *was* aerial surveillance.

11. The combination ~~of these tracking techniques~~ ~~were~~ *was* very helpful in ensuring the wolves' survival.

12. However, in 2008 the wolves in Wyoming, Idaho, and Montana were removed from federal protection.

13. Since then, a coalition of wildlife and environmental groups have objected to the wolves' removal from the endangered species list.

14. According to state authorities, a target population of 150 wolves per state are enough to ensure the wolves' survival.

15. However, environmentalists argue that this number of wolves are far too small.

16. Fortunately, there are another group of people supporting the wolves—the Nez Perce Indian tribe in Idaho.

17. The traditions of this tribe is strongly linked to the gray wolf, which once roamed freely throughout the territory that is now the Nez Perce reservation.

18. One of the tribe's projects involve importing wild wolves from Canada and releasing them in Idaho.

19. Another of the tribe's projects are a device called the Howlbox, which is being developed at the University of Montana.

20. The purpose of Howlboxes are to provide a less expensive way of tracking wolves than putting collars on individual animals.

21. The function of the Howlboxes is to emit a wolf howl each morning and evening and to record any answering calls from the wolves.

22. When the wolves in the vicinity hear the howl, each of them howl back.

23. Every one of the wolves have a unique howl, so scientists can distinguish one wolf's howls from another's.

24. The total number ~~of different individual~~ howls give [gives] biologists an estimate of how many wolves are ~~in the area.~~

25. The cost of trapping individual wolves and ~~of attaching~~ radio collars ~~to them~~ are [is] $1500 per wolf, and it costs an additional $1000 per year to track each wolf's location.

26. A single Howlbox costs $1300, but even one ~~of the boxes~~ are [is] able ~~to track~~ a large number of wolves.

27. A Howlbox is typically placed ~~in a tree for several days,~~ and after a few days ~~of recording~~ the wolves ~~in that area,~~ each ~~of the boxes~~ are [is] moved to a new location ~~to record~~ other wolves.

28. The Nez Perce tribe, along ~~with officials of the United States, Fish and Wildlife Service,~~ are [is] working hard ~~to ensure~~ the survival ~~of the gray wolf in Idaho.~~

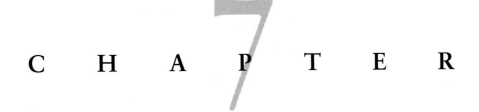

C H A P T E R 7

SUBJECTS UNDERSTOOD
IN A SPECIAL SENSE

This chapter discusses several small groups of words used as subjects that call for special attention in subject–verb agreement.

Rule 6. Some subjects, though **plural in form,** are **singular in meaning** and, therefore, require a singular verb. Such words include *news, mathematics, physics, economics, aeronautics, electronics, molasses, mumps,* and *measles.*

Economics was my least favorite class.

Mumps is a common disease among children.

Rule 7. A **unit of time, weight, measurement, distance,** or **money** usually requires a singular verb because the entire amount is thought of as a single unit.

Twenty *dollars is* all the money I have.

Two *pounds* of meat *feeds* four people.

Eighteen *yards* of cloth *completes* our fabric needs.

Rule 8. Collective nouns usually require singular verbs. A collective noun is a word that is singular in form but that refers to a group of people or things. Some common collective nouns are such words as *group, team, family, class, crowd,* and *committee.*

The *crowd is* very noisy.

The *committee holds* frequent meetings.

Occasionally, a collective noun may be used with a plural verb if the writer wishes to show that the members of the group are acting as separate individuals rather than as a unified body. Notice the difference in meaning between the following pair of sentences:

The *board of directors supports* the measure. (In this sentence, the *board of directors* is acting as a single, unified group.)

The *board of directors are divided* over whether to pass the measure. (In this sentence, *the board of directors* is viewed as a collection of separate individuals who, because they are not in agreement, are not acting as a unified group.)

EXERCISE 7A

Part 1: Circle the verb that correctly completes each sentence. This section of the exercise covers only the rules from Chapter 7.

1. Mumps (makes, **make**) it difficult for a person to swallow.

2. Two weeks (is, **are**) not enough time to visit six different countries.

3. Sixty pounds (seems, **seem**) like a lot of weight to lose in one year.

4. Measles (**kills**, kill) many children in poor areas of the world.

5. The jury (**has**, have) agreed to sentence the defendant to life in prison.

6. According to the defendant's attorney, twenty-five years in prison (**is**, are) a more reasonable sentence.

7. Economics (studies, **study**) the ways people accumulate wealth.

8. The evening news (**summarizes**, summarize) the major events of the day.

Part 2: The following sentences cover rules from Chapters 5–7. They describe the efforts of a recent college graduate to find housing in the city where she will soon be starting a new job. Circle the verb that correctly completes each sentence.

9. Among Sarah's immediate tasks (is, **are**) finding a place to live.

10. Ten days (**is**, are) all the time she has to find an apartment and to get moved in.

11. One of her biggest problems (**is**, ~~are~~) locating something affordable.

12. Fifteen hundred dollars a month (**is**, are) all she can afford to spend on rent.

13. Most of the apartments in her city (charges, **charge**) higher rents.

14. A list of available apartments from a rental agency (**gives**, give) Sarah some choices to consider.

15. Each of the one-bedroom apartments on her list (rents, rent) for more than two thousand dollars a month.

16. A less expensive alternative (is, are) studio apartments, with no separate bedroom.

17. Some of the studio apartments (falls, fall) within Sarah's price range.

18. Everyone (advises, advise) her to live by herself rather than trying to rent a larger place with a roommate.

19. According to her friends, the disadvantages of sharing an apartment with a stranger (outweighs, outweigh) the financial advantages of splitting the rent with another person.

20. One of the studio apartments (comes, come) with a reserved parking space.

21. Included in the rent for another studio apartment (is, are) access to the complex's swimming pool and exercise room.

22. A spacious kitchen with a brand-new stove and refrigerator (makes, make) a third apartment appealing to Sarah.

23. Also important to Sarah (is, are) the distances between these apartments and her office.

24. She likes the apartment with the pool, but forty-five minutes (is, are) a long time to drive in city traffic twice each day.

25. Neither of the other two studio apartments (requires, require) such a long commute.

26. Each of the three apartments (appeals, appeal) to Sarah, so she will need to think carefully before making her final decision.

EXERCISE 7B

Some of the sentences in this exercise contain one or more subject-verb agreement errors. Others are correct as written. If a sentence contains a subject-verb agreement error, cross out the incorrect verb and write the correct form in its place. If the sentence has no agreement errors, mark it *C* for *correct*. This exercise covers rules from Chapters 5–7.

1. My niece Ellen has just earned her master's degree, and there is some major career decisions facing her.

2. A degree from a well-known university, together with her extensive work experience, make her an attractive job candidate.

3. She has received job offers from companies in several different states, and each of the potential jobs appeal to her in some way.

4. Among the most important factors for Ellen are a good salary.

5. Of course, everyone want to get paid well, but financial security is especially important to Ellen.

6. Her main financial obligation are her student loans.

7. Six years are a long time to attend college, and the tuition at an Ivy League university has left her with a forty-thousand-dollar debt.

8. The interest rate on her loans vary from 5 to 8 percent.

9. After she leaves school, six months are all the time Ellen has before she must start to repay her loans.

10. Among Ellen's other concerns are job satisfaction.

11. For beginning employees in her field, fifty hours a week constitute a normal workload.

12. Because she will have to spend long hours at the office, a combination of interesting work and a comfortable job environment are high on Ellen's list of priorities.

13. One of her potential jobs pay very well, but the suburban location of its offices do not appeal to Ellen.

14. Ellen has always lived in large cities, and an urban location with many cultural activities is important to her.

15. Most of her free time are spent attending concerts and plays or visiting art galleries and museums.

16. Ellen is single, and a family with a husband and several children figure prominently in her plans for the future.

17. For Ellen, another advantage of urban life are the large numbers of single professional people she can meet.

18. She faces many decisions, and each of them have the potential to alter the course of her future.

19. Her whole family are watching to see what she decides to do.

EXERCISE 8B

Some of the sentences in this exercise contain subject-verb agreement errors. Others are correct as written. If a sentence contains a subject-verb agreement error, cross out the incorrect verb, and write the correct form in its place. If a sentence has no agreement errors, label it *C* for *correct*. This exercise covers the rules from Chapters 5–8.

1. Some of the ancient world's systems for predicting the future or for analyzing an individual's personality is still in use today.

2. One of these ancient systems are numerology.

3. There are different forms of numerology, but each of them believe that a relationship exists between numbers and physical objects and between numbers and living things.

4. In one system of numerology, everything in the universe vibrate at its own frequency.

5. The frequency of an object's vibrations establish the qualities associated with it.

6. Either a person's name or the combination of his name and birth date become the basis for an analysis of his character.

7. How do names or a birth date become a number with numerological significance?

8. Every one of the letters in the alphabet get a specific numerical value, ranging from one through nine.

9. Because there are twenty-six letters and only nine numbers, some of the letters has the same numerical value.

10. The sequence of numbers in a person's name or birth date are then reduced to a single digit.

11. For example, the number 2216 becomes $2 + 2 + 1 + 6$, and this sequence of numbers is further reduced to 11 and then to $1 + 1 = 2$.

12. Each of the numbers from one through nine have specific personality qualities associated with it.

13. Among the qualities associated with the number two is cooperation and harmony.

14. In some forms of numerology, a certain number or a combination of numbers brings either good or bad luck to a particular object.

15. For example, to the Chinese one of the luckiest numbers are ninety-nine.

16. The number nine means "long life," so putting two 9s together means "eternity."

17. If you go to Southern California's Chinese American communities, a common sight are signs advertising the 99 Ranch Market chain of stores.

18. A wide selection of Asian grocery products and an emphasis on selling very fresh vegetables and seafood probably accounts for the enormous success of these markets.

19. However, to a believer in numerology, the number 99 in the name of the stores also play an important role.

20. Some of the people who buy lottery tickets believes in lucky numbers.

21. A combination of his three grandchildren's birth dates are what one gambler bets on week after week.

22. A horoscope column in a newspaper or a slip of paper in a fortune cookie also provide a list of lucky numbers.

23. Does the ability of numbers to affect people and events seem logical to you?

24. Each of us have to make decisions about what is real and what is superstition.

UNIT 2 REVIEW

Correct any subject-verb agreement errors that you find in the following paragraphs by crossing out the incorrect verbs and writing in the correct forms. It may help you to underline all the subjects in the sentences *once* and the verbs *twice* before you try to identify the errors in agreement.

Mark and Debbie Cooper are planning a vacation in Hawaii on Waikiki Beach. A collection of maps and tour brochures are spread across their dining room table. Each of the brochures offer a different tour package. The variety of hotels and airlines seem bewildering. There are many choices, but only a few of the choices fit the Coopers' budget and time limits. The Coopers can spend six days on their vacation, and six days are not enough time for them to see everything they want to.

Among the more expensive hotels are the Hilton Hawaiian Village on Waikiki Beach. Its beachfront location and its many extra amenities makes this hotel very popular with tourists. Its combination of eighteen restaurants and more than ninety shops provide guests with plenty of places to eat and spend money. There are also a wide variety of recreational activities. A kayak ride or surfing lessons are popular ocean activities for the hotel's guests. A boogie board or an aqua cycle give guests other ways to enjoy the sea. In addition to the ocean, each of the hotel's five pools provide more opportunities for swimming and getting a suntan. Among other special activities are a traditional Hawaiian luau every Friday with Polynesian dancing and a fireworks show.

Because they are on a tight budget, the Coopers think they might be better off choosing a less expensive Hawaiian tour package. Each of these tours include round-trip airfare and a hotel room. Most of the tour packages also provide use of a rental car. One of the tours offer discount coupons for local shops.

The type of hotel room vary with each tour package. Some of the hotel rooms includes a kitchenette. The cost of meals are a major concern for the Coopers. Waikiki is a resort area, and the price of restaurant meals there are very expensive. Thirty-five dollars a day are all the Coopers want to spend on food. Being able to prepare some of their own meals in their hotel room could save them a lot of money.

Among their other expenses is parking fees. Fifteen dollars a day is the usual charge for hotel parking. Either free parking or a room with a kitchenette are necessary for the Coopers. They haven't been able to find a hotel that offers both.

Distance from the beach isn't very important to the Coopers. They realize that the price of beachfront hotels are more than they can afford. Two or three blocks don't seem too long a distance for them to walk to the beach. After all, the sunshine and the fresh ocean air makes walking in Waikiki a pleasure.

According to the travel brochures, "Here in Waikiki are everything you need for a wonderful tropical vacation." Although they will have to plan their trip carefully, the Coopers are looking forward to their six days in Hawaii.

UNIT 3

Identifying and Punctuating the Main Types of Sentences

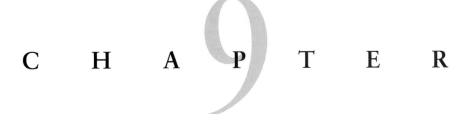

C H A P T E R 9

COMPOUND SENTENCES

 compound sentence, a very common sentence pattern, contains *at least two subjects and two verbs,* usually arranged in an S–V/S–V pattern. For example,

   S   V   S   V
Bob wrecked his car last week, and now he rides the bus to work.

   S   V   S   V
Nina lived in Italy for two years, so she speaks Italian fluently.

In grammar, the term **compound** means "having two or more parts." Thus, a sentence may have a **compound subject,** for example, "The *husband* and his *wife* were at the opera." Or, a sentence may have a **compound verb,** for example, "The man *rode* his bike and *sped* down the street." Do not confuse a sentence with a **compound subject** or a **compound verb** with a **compound sentence.**

A compound sentence can be divided into two parts, each of which can be a separate sentence by itself.

Bob wrecked his car last week.   +   Now he rides the bus to work.

Nina lived in Italy for two years.   +   She speaks Italian very fluently.

Because a compound sentence can be divided into *two* separate sentences, each half of a compound sentence must contain at least one subject and one verb. Therefore, each half of a compound sentence is a **clause.** A clause is a group of words that contains both a subject and a verb. (In contrast, a group of words that does not contain both a subject and a verb is called a **phrase,** as in a prepositional phrase.) A clause that can stand alone as a complete sentence is called an **independent clause.** Because each clause in a compound sentence can stand alone as a complete sentence, each clause must be independent. In other words,

A compound sentence consists of at least two independent clauses joined together to form a single sentence.

There are two ways to join independent clauses to form a compound sentence. The most frequently used method is to put a conjunction between the clauses. A **conjunction** is a word that joins words or groups of words. In grammar, the word *coordinate* means "of equal importance." Therefore, the conjunctions that are used in compound sentences are called **coordinating conjunctions** because they join two groups of words that are of equal grammatical importance. (They are both independent clauses.) The following coordinating conjunctions are used to join the clauses of compound sentences:

and

but

for (when it means *because*)

nor

or

so

yet

You should *memorize* these coordinating conjunctions because later you will have to be able to distinguish between them and the connecting words that are used to form other kinds of sentences.

Some students use the following made-up word to help them remember coordinating conjunctions:

F	A	N	B	O	Y	S
for	and	nor	but	or	yet	so

In the following sentences, underline the subjects of the compound sentences *once* and the verbs *twice,* and circle the coordinating conjunction that joins the clauses. Notice that a comma *precedes* the coordinating conjunction.

The president entered the room, and the band began to play "Hail to the Chief."

She diets constantly, but her weight remains the same.

I rarely prepare casseroles, for my family refuses to eat them.

We must hurry, or we will miss the first part of the movie.

He can't help you, nor can I.

(Notice that when the conjunction *nor* is used to join two independent clauses, the pattern becomes S–V/V–S: My coat isn't here, nor is my hat.)

The defendant was ill, so the trial was postponed.

He earns only $800 a month, yet he lives quite comfortably.

Construct compound sentences of your own, using the coordinating conjunctions listed below to join your clauses. Underline the subject of each clause *once* and the verb *twice.* (You may construct a clause that has more than one subject and/or more than one verb, but each clause must have *at least* one subject and one verb.)

_____ , and _____

_____ , but _____

_____ , for _____

_____ , or _____

2. The second way to join the clauses in a compound sentence is to use a semicolon (;) *in place of both the comma and the coordinating conjunction.* For example,

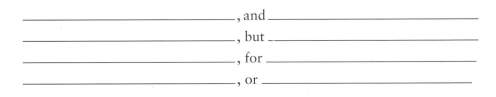

She could not find her keys; they must have fallen somewhere.

Mark is always late for work; he oversleeps every morning.

Compound sentences constructed with semicolons occur less frequently than compound sentences constructed with coordinating conjunctions because some type of connecting word is usually needed to show the relationship between the clauses. For example, without a coordinating conjunction the logical relationship between the two clauses in the following sentence might be confusing.

> My grandfather has lived in the United States for fifty years; he has never learned to speak English.

If, however, you replace the semicolon with a coordinating conjunction, the relationship between the clauses becomes clear.

> My grandfather has lived in the United States for fifty years, but he has never learned to speak English.

It is all right to use the semicolon by itself between the clauses of a compound sentence, but do so only when the relationship between the clauses is clear without a connecting word.

2. Construct two compound sentences of your own, using semicolons to join the clauses. Underline the subjects *once* and the verbs *twice*. Make certain that each clause has at least one subject and one verb.

_____ ; _____

_____ ; _____

3. Another common way to show the relationship between the clauses of a compound sentence is to use a **conjunctive adverb,** such as *however,* in the second clause. Notice that a *semicolon* is required between the clauses. A comma follows the conjunctive adverb.

> We all studied quite hard; however, the test was more difficult than we had expected.

Conjunctive adverbs are especially frequent in formal language, in which expressing the precise relationship between ideas is the goal. Here are the most frequently used conjunctive adverbs:

also	furthermore	indeed
anyway	hence	instead
besides	however	likewise
consequently	in addition	meanwhile
finally	incidentally	moreover

1. and, or, but   2.

$\underline{S+V}$, $\underline{S+V}$ $\underline{S+V}$; $\underline{S+V}$

nevertheless	otherwise	therefore
next	still	thus
nonetheless	then	

A conjunctive adverb gets its double name from the fact that it does two things at once: It connects, like other **conjunctions,** and it modifies, like other **adverbs.** Because it is adverbial, it can be located in many places in its own clause. Because it can move around in the second clause and does not always come *exactly between* the two clauses (like coordinating conjunctions), it does not necessarily act as a signal to readers that they are coming to the second half of a compound sentence. For these reasons, the strong signal of a semicolon marks the end of the first clause.

Bob loved to surf; therefore, he lived near the beach.

Joe, however, liked to hike; he lived near the mountains.

Notice that the conjunctive adverb is always "set off" with a comma, or two commas, in its own clause. Construct three compound sentences of your own that use conjunctive adverbs. Try putting the conjunctive adverb in several different places in the second clause.

1. _____

2. _____

3. _____

(Did you remember to "set off" the conjunctive adverb with one or two commas?)

As you can see from the sentences that you have constructed in this lesson, the following punctuation rules apply to compound sentences:

1. If the clauses in a compound sentence are joined by a coordinating conjunction, place a comma *before* (to the left of) the conjunction.

This sentence is compound, and it contains a comma.

You may have learned that it is not necessary to use commas in short compound sentences (for example, "He's a Scorpio and I'm a Libra."). Although this is true, not everyone agrees on how short a "short" compound sentence is, so if you are in doubt, it is safer to use a comma. All the sentences in the exercises for this unit will be "long" compound sentences and should have a comma before the conjunction.

2. Although a compound sentence may contain more than one coordinating conjunction, the comma is placed before the conjunction that joins the clauses.

Jan and I attended the same college, and now we work for the same company.

3. If the clauses in a compound sentence are *not* joined by a coordinating conjunction, place a semicolon between the clauses. If the clauses are joined by a conjunctive adverb, the adverb must also be *followed* by a comma.

I don't have my book with me; I must have left it at home.
We hurried to the theater; however, the film was over.

The following sentence patterns do *not* require commas because they are simple (meaning that they contain only one clause) rather than compound.

S–V–V	He ordered a baked potato but was served French fries instead. (no comma)
S–S–V	My uncle and aunt live in Boston. (no comma)
S–S–V–V	My cousin and I went to England and stayed there for two months. (no comma)

To review, the three patterns for punctuating a compound sentence are:
independent clause + comma + coordinating conjunction + independent clause

We went to a play, and next we had some dinner.

independent clause + semicolon + independent clause

We didn't enjoy the movie; it was boring.

independent clause + semicolon + conjunctive adverb + comma + independent clause

I love to draw; however, I have little artistic talent.

EXERCISE 9A

Add <u>commas</u> and <u>semicolons</u> to the following sentences wherever they are needed. If a sentence needs no additional punctuation (in other words, if the sentence is simple rather than compound), label it C for *correct*.

1. The year 2009 was the five hundredth anniversary of the birth of England's King Henry VIII, so people in Britain planned many special events to commemorate his reign. *coordinating conjunction*

2. One exhibit focused on the king's many wives for Henry VIII was married six times.

3. His first wife was Catherine of Aragon she was a princess from Spain.

4. Catherine had been married to Henry's older brother however he died shortly after their marriage.

5. During her marriage to Henry, Catherine gave birth to eight children nevertheless only a single daughter lived past infancy.

6. Henry wanted a male heir to succeed him on his throne and he became discouraged at Catherine's failure to produce a son.

7. He had to find a new wife otherwise he might never have a male heir.

8. The Catholic Church refused to grant Henry a divorce; therefore, *(CA)* Henry made himself the head of a new English church, independent of Rome.

9. Henry then divorced Catherine and married a beautiful young English woman, Anne Boleyn.

10. Anne was already pregnant at the time of their marriage, *CC* but she also gave birth to a daughter.

11. Anne then became pregnant with a son however this pregnancy ended in a miscarriage.

12. Henry now wanted an excuse to divorce his second wife so he accused her of being unfaithful to him, a capital crime.

13. Anne Boleyn was executed thus Henry was now free to marry his third wife, Jane Seymour.

14. Jane Seymour gave birth to a son but died shortly after the baby's birth.

15. Henry's fourth marriage was political he married a Protestant German noble-woman, Anne of Cleves.

16. Henry had never met Anne before their marriage and he was shocked by her appearance.

17. Henry made no secret of his disappointment with Anne he described her in public as "the mare (female horse) of Flanders."

18. Their marriage in January of 1540 was never consummated consequently it was possible for Henry to get the marriage annulled in July.

19. Henry was much older than his young and flirtatious fifth wife and Catherine Howard had love affairs with younger men throughout her marriage to Henry.

20. She was executed for high treason therefore Henry was once again free to remarry.

21. He made a wiser choice for his sixth wife for this time he was looking for a step-mother for the three children from his first three marriages.

22. Catherine Parr had already been widowed twice so she took a very practical view of her marriage to Henry in 1543.

23. She did not expect to have a romantic marriage with Henry nor was she interested in having love affairs of her own.

24. Her primary duties were to care for an aging Henry and to be a mother to his children.

25. Catherine was widowed for a third time by Henry's death in 1547 yet this was not the last of her marriages.

26. A year later, Catherine married for the fourth time however she died in childbirth the following year.

27. Henry's many wives are hard for English schoolchildren to remember so they use the following rhyme to recall the fates of these six women: "Divorced, executed, died; annulled, executed, survived."

EXERCISE 9B

Add commas and semicolons to the following sentences wherever they are needed. If a sentence needs no additional punctuation (in other words, if the sentence is simple rather than compound), label it *C* for *correct*.

1. Most of us listen to rock and roll or jazz and we may also enjoy a little bit of Broadway show music, like the songs from *Wicked*.

2. The appeal of opera may seem more limited however there are thousands of people in love with opera.

3. These loyal fans sometimes travel all over the world to follow their favorite operas from one opera house to another.

4. The great nineteenth-century German composer Richard Wagner attracts such followers for fans ~~of his opera~~ will show up ~~in Los Angeles or San Francisco or New York or even Bayreuth, Germany.~~

5. Wagner wanted a special festival to showcase his works and chose Bayreuth as the site.

6. Wagner originally wanted to have a site for his great Ring cycle operas and his opera *Parsifal* but soon all of his operas were being performed there.

7. Fans today of Wagner's operas may have to wait for years to obtain tickets to this festival nevertheless they don't mind the lengthy wait.

8. The site of this pilgrimage has its own unique history and reflects Richard Wagner's powerful originality.

9. Artists traditionally have been funded by patrons or they have gained support from governments.

10. King Ludwig II of Bavaria gave the majority of money for the construction of Wagner's amazing theater but Wagner controlled every aspect of its creation.

11. Wagner even supervised the design and construction of the theater for he wanted the theater to accommodate a huge orchestra and his unique ideas about staging.

12. Unlike typical nineteenth-century buildings, the exterior of the theater is modest and mostly undecorated.

13. Wagner wanted the architecture of his theater to help convey the spirit of his operas so he changed two important features of orchestra staging.

14. His unusual orchestra pit broke with tradition for it is recessed under the stage and covered by a hood.

15. Wagner did not want the audience to be distracted from the drama onstage by the conductor's movements or by the orchestra.

16. Another of Wagner's changes was to double the archway near the front of the stage this causes the stage to appear more distant.

17. Wagner wanted to create a "mystic gulf" between the audience and the stage and the doubling of the arch and the darkened, recessed orchestra pit help to create this impression.

18. Wagner's operas use myth for their story therefore he wanted the architecture of his theater to give a distant, dreamlike character to his performances.

19. The theater is very special however conductors find its unique architecture very difficult to work in.

20. The orchestra and the conductor perform in darkness and the building's acoustic reverberation makes it difficult to synchronize the orchestra with the singers.

21. Even the world's greatest conductors speak of the struggle and challenge of working in this theater.

22. The foundation stone for the building was laid on Wagner's birthday on May 22, 1872 and four years later the building opened for the premier of the complete four-opera cycle of *The Ring of the Nibelung* on August 13, 1876.

23. Clearly, all types of music have their devoted fans but Wagner's fans may be the most devoted.

24. Thousands of these fans travel every year to Germany to hear Wagner's operas performed at this unique site.

EXERCISE 9C

Part One: Make each item a compound sentence by adding 1) a clause of your own and 2) the correct punctuation.

1. I got up an hour late **so**

2. I got up an hour late **nevertheless**

3. I may buy a new car this summer **or**

4. Jim never graduated from high school **however**

Part Two: Combine each pair of sentences into a single compound sentence by adding 1) a conjunction and 2) the correct punctuation.

    a. Write out the whole new sentence on the blank line.

    b. You must use *a different* conjunction in each sentence.

5. Sam and Susan wanted to have a baby.

Susan was not able to become pregnant.

_____

6. Susan had an operation to help her become pregnant.

She became pregnant six months later.

_____

7. After this operation, a woman may have just one baby.

She may have several babies.

_____

8. Susan gave birth to triplets.

She and Sam were now the parents of three boys.

_____

When he comes over, *we watch television.*

If we come to the play, _____

_____

Before we saw the movie, _____

_____

You have now constructed two complex sentences. A **complex sentence** contains both independent and dependent clauses. (In contrast, a **compound sentence** contains only *independent* clauses.)

Every dependent clause begins with a subordinating conjunction. A **conjunction** joins words or groups of words. The conjunctions that begin dependent clauses are called **subordinating conjunctions** because the word *subordinate* means "of lesser importance." Grammatically speaking, a dependent clause is "less important" than an independent clause because it cannot stand alone as a complete sentence. In contrast, the conjunctions that you used in the previous lesson to form compound sentences are called **coordinating conjunctions** because *coordinate* means "of equal importance." Because both of the clauses in a compound sentence are independent, both clauses are "of equal importance."

The type of dependent clause that you will be studying in this lesson is called an **adverb clause** because, like other adverbs, an adverb clause describes a verb (or sometimes an adjective or an adverb). It is the same kind of clause that you worked with in Chapter 2. The subordinating conjunctions used to begin adverb clauses describe verbs by telling *how, when, where, why,* or *under what conditions* the action occurs.

how: as if, as though

when: after, as, as soon as, before, until, when, whenever, while

where: where, wherever

why: because, in order that, since, so that

under what conditions: although, as long as, even though, if, though, unless

Read the following sentences. A slanted line indicates the point at which each sentence divides into two separate clauses. Underline the subject of each clause *once* and the verb *twice.* Circle the subordinating conjunction.

While we studied, / he watched television.

I babysat / so that they could go to a movie.

As long as we communicate, / we will remain friends.

Now examine the clause in each sentence that contains the circled subordinating conjunction.

The clause that contains the subordinating conjunction is the dependent clause.

Notice that in a complex sentence, the dependent clause may be either the first or the second clause in the sentence.

When Joe wants to relax, he goes fishing.

Rick finds time to exercise *after he finishes work.*

In most cases, the adverb clauses in a complex sentence are *reversible.* That is, the sentence has the same basic meaning no matter which clause comes first. For example,

While he is on the train, he usually reads his books.

He usually reads his books *while he is on the train.*

or

If we go on vacation, we will have lots of fun.

We will have lots of fun *if we go on vacation.*

However, the order of the clauses in a complex sentence does affect the punctuation of the sentence.

1. If the **dependent** clause is the first clause in the sentence, it is followed by a comma.

    Before she performed at the club, Stephanie welcomed her guests.

2. If the **independent** clause is the first clause in the sentence, no comma is needed.

    Stephanie welcomed her guests *before she performed at the club.*

Punctuate the following complex sentences. First circle the subordinating conjunction in each sentence, and draw a slanted line between the clauses.

After we eat dinner we're going to see a movie.

The child carries her teddy bear with her wherever she goes.

If it doesn't rain the crops will be ruined.

As soon as I finish painting my apartment I'll help you paint yours.

EXERCISE 10A

The following sentences are **complex.** First, underline the dependent clause in each sentence. Then, add a comma if it is necessary. If a sentence needs no additional punctuation, label it *C* for *correct.*

1. Although few people have heard of Joseph Glidden his invention changed the history of the Old West.

2. When Americans think of the Old West they picture cowboys and Indians riding across miles of open range.

3. This scene changed after large numbers of farmers and ranchers began to settle on the plains.

4. These settlers needed to build fences so that they could mark the boundaries of their property and protect their livestock and their crops.

5. Unless their land was fenced ranchers could not keep their livestock from running away.

6. Farmers could not protect their crops from roaming animals until they built fences.

7. When people in other parts of the United States built fences they used wood rails or large stones.

8. Because the West had a very limited supply of trees and large rocks settlers there had a hard time finding material for their fences.

9. Although they tried to raise thorny hedges for fences the hedges took years to grow.

10. Wire fences did not work because a single strand of wire was not strong enough to restrain a herd of animals on the run.

11. The fencing problem was solved when Joseph Glidden invented barbed wire in 1874.

12. Glidden's wire was stronger than ordinary wire because it had sharp steel barbs.

13. Even though animals often tried to break through ordinary wire fences they quickly learned to avoid touching the painful barbed wire.

14. Glidden also invented machinery to mass-produce his barbed wire so that he could sell it at a cheap price.

15. Because settlers now had an effective and inexpensive way to fence their land miles of barbed wire soon stretched across the West.

16. Wherever there were barbed-wire fences the open range came to an end.

17. After he invented barbed wire Glidden became one of the wealthiest men in the United States.

18. When he died his fortune was estimated at a million dollars.

19. If you travel to the city of LaCrosse, Kansas you will find a whole museum devoted to barbed wire.

20. While you are at the museum you can see a life-size diorama of a cowboy repairing a barbed-wire fence under a moon-lit sky.

21. Looking at the diorama makes you feel as though you were back on a cattle ranch in the Old West.

22. If Joseph Glidden were alive today he would still see his barbed-wire fences in use throughout the western and southwestern United States.

Exercise 10B

The following exercise includes simple, compound, and complex sentences. Add commas and semicolons wherever they are needed. If a sentence is simple and needs no additional punctuation, label it C for *correct*.

1. Whenever we turn on our computers to connect to the Internet we have the opportunity to become a part of a changing world of business and even of journalism.

2. For example, many people go online to check opinions of other consumers when they are thinking about buying a new product.

3. These opinions and responses are called "consumer generated media" and they are part of a whole new Internet world.

4. In the recent past, these opinions could have been an e-mail post to friends or an online letter on a company website but online posting has changed and become much more widespread and powerful.

5. If you have participated in an Internet forum, kept your own blog, or responded to someone's blogs then you are part of consumer generated media.

6. Although we tend to think of our consumer comments only in terms of writing consumer generated media also includes video, audio, and multimedia posts created by consumers.

7. Consumer generated media includes all these kinds of responses because the Internet is open to everyone and anyone.

8. While some multimedia posts may be in support of a particular product, brand, or corporate institution others may be negative parodies or strong protests.

9. The freedom of access of the Internet makes it impossible for companies to control consumer reactions even though these companies may spend millions of dollars on advertisements.

10. If a product or a company has problems consumer generated media will get the message out.

11. The Internet is changing our lives so that news is not just something in a newspaper, on a radio, or on a television newscast.

12. Because the Internet allows average citizens to participate in all aspects of journalism many people call citizen journalism a new, exciting form of democracy.

13. In this new form of journalism, you and I can participate in several ways because the Internet offers so many options.

14. People can add comments to printed news stories and they can also add their own stories and pictures to blogs and personal broadcasting sites.

15. Since citizen journalism allows people without professional journalism training to use the tools of modern technology individuals can blog about a city council meeting or fact-check a newspaper article or post a digital photo or video on YouTube about an event.

16. Because the CNN and Fox news websites offer easy links for anyone to add pictures and videos many people have been encouraged to participate and provide eyewitness accounts.

17. Such eyewitness accounts are actually broadcast on the air so that individuals receive acknowledgment of their citizen journalism.

18. Before the Internet, none of this would have been possible even though people have always called news departments with "tips" about stories.

19. Many news editors welcome these found contributions from their viewers so new citizen journalism is now a big part of news.

20. If you thought citizen journalism occurred only in the United States you are very mistaken.

21. In South Korea, OhmyNews, with its motto of "Every Citizen Is a Reporter," is a popular form of citizen journalism and it has had substantial influence on South Korea's politics.

22. Wherever there is access to the Internet there is the possibility for any one of us to contribute to the world of journalism and information.

EXERCISE 10C

Part One: Make each item a complex sentence by adding 1) a clause of your own and 2) the correct punctuation.

1. **After** this semester ends

2. _____ **even though** he doesn't have

   much money.

3. **Because** the automobile factory plans to lay off hundreds of workers

4. **Whenever** I need to relax

5. My sister is moving to New York **so that**

6. _____ **until** I graduate from college.

7. **Although** our boss promised to give us a 10 percent raise

8. **As soon as** _____ we can leave for our

   vacation.

9. **If** you want to save some money

Part Two: Write your own complex sentences, following the directions in each item. Be sure to punctuate the sentences correctly.

10. Write a complex sentence about someone in your family, using the conjunction *because.*

11. Write a complex sentence about something that happened to you in the past, using the conjunction *although.*

12. Write a complex sentence about something you may do in the future, using the conjunction *if.*

13. Write a sentence about something that happened to you last week, using the conjunction *when*.

14. Write a complex sentence using the conjunction *before*.

15. Write a complex sentence using the conjunction *while*.

CHAPTER 11

AVOIDING RUN-ON SENTENCES AND COMMA SPLICES

As you learned in Chapter 9, a compound sentence consists of at least two independent clauses. The independent clauses in a compound sentence must be separated either by a coordinating conjunction (such as *and, but, or*) preceded by a comma or by a semicolon if no conjunction is used.

Failure to separate two independent clauses results in an error known as a **run-on sentence.** The following are examples of run-on sentences:

I don't play tennis well I have a poor backhand.

The next game is at our school we want to go to it.

Run-on sentences are very serious errors. They are not only confusing to the reader but also indicate that the writer cannot tell where one sentence ends and another begins.

There are three ways to correct a run-on sentence.

1. Divide the run-on into two separate sentences, ending each with a period. (If the sentences are questions, end them with question marks.)

I don't play tennis well. I have a poor backhand.

The next game is at our school. We want to go to it.

Although this method produces grammatically correct sentences, an essay written completely in such short, simple sentences creates the choppy effect of an elementary school reading text. Therefore, you should also consider using the two other methods of correcting run-ons.

2. Change the run-on to a **compound sentence** by separating the clauses with a coordinating conjunction, a conjunctive adverb, or just a semicolon if the relationship between the clauses is clear without a conjunction.

I don't play tennis well, *for* I have a poor backhand.

or

I have a poor backhand; *as a result,* I don't play tennis well.

or

I don't play tennis well; I have a poor backhand.
The next game is at our school, *so* we want to go to it.

or

The next game is at our school; *therefore,* we want to go to it.

or

The next game is at our school; we want to go to it.

As you learned previously, the relationship between the two clauses in a compound sentence is often clearer if a conjunction is used rather than a semicolon.

3. Change the run-on to a complex sentence by placing a subordinating conjunction before one of the clauses.

I don't play tennis well *because* I have a poor backhand.

Because the next game is at our school, we want to go to it.

Another very common error is the comma splice. Unlike a run-on, in which two independent clauses are run together with no punctuation, a **comma splice** consists of two independent clauses joined with *not enough* punctuation—that is, with only a comma (and *no* coordinating conjunction). The following are examples of comma splices:

She is a full-time student, she works forty hours a week.

Bob needs a new car, he can't afford to buy one now.

A comma by itself is *not* a strong enough punctuation mark to separate two independent clauses. Only periods and semicolons can be used without conjunctions to separate independent clauses. Comma splices can be corrected by the same three methods used for correcting run-on sentences.

1. Divide the comma splice into two separate sentences.

   Sue is a full-time student. She works forty hours a week.

   Bob needs a new car. He can't afford to buy one now.

2. Change the comma splice into a **compound sentence** by separating the clauses with either a coordinating conjunction, conjunctive adverb, or just a semicolon if the relationship between the two clauses is clear without a conjunction.

   Sue is a full-time student, *and* she works forty hours a week.

   or

   Sue is a full-time student; *in addition,* she works forty hours a week.

   Bob needs a new car, *but* he can't afford to buy one now.

   or

   Bob needs a new car; *however,* he can't afford to buy one now.

3. Change the comma splice into a **complex sentence** by placing a subordinating conjunction before one of the clauses.

   Even though Sue is a full-time student, she works forty hours a week.

   Although Bob needs a new car, he can't afford to buy one now.

Remember that if the dependent clause (the clause continuing the subordinating conjunction) is the first clause in the sentence, it should be followed by a comma.

Correct the following run-on sentences and comma splices:

I would like to visit Hawaii I have many relatives there.

All my sisters have blue eyes I do not.

Gary grew up in Minnesota, he is used to cold weather.

They are always in debt they have too many credit cards.

Exercise 11B

The following essay contains run-on sentences and comma splices. Correct these errors, using the methods you have learned in this and previous chapters.

Just about everyone loves comics, they appeal to both children and adults. We usually think of comics as being humorous however their subject matter now includes all types of materials.

A defining feature of comics is their sequential nature. The story or narrative is told through a series of pictures with dialogue attached. The dialogue can be in captions it is usually put into word balloons. A comprehensive definition of the term "comics" has been provided by Will Eisner, he is known as the "father of the graphic novel." Eisner defines comics as pictures or images and words arranged to narrate a story or to dramatize an idea. This definition includes traditional comics strips and comic books, it includes newer forms like web comics and graphic novels. Graphic novels are full-length stories told in comic-strip form. Their content may be humorous, it is often serious.

The history of comics has a lot to do with the history of print technology. One of the first works to be identified as a comic form was William Hogarth's 1726 work called *A Rake's Progress*. It consisted of eight painted canvases depicting the adventures of a young man in London. He comes to London as a rich man he ends up in a debtor's prison. Each canvas was reproduced as a print together they created a story. Comics did not become widely read until the nineteenth century, by this time print technologies allowed mass publication of newspapers and magazines. In 1841 a British magazine called *Punch* published satirical political drawings, by 1843 these drawings had received the name of "cartoons." In the 1920s and 1930s, color comic strips printed on sheets of newsprint were sold at newsstands these comics were called *The Funnies*. In 1938 Action Comics introduced the first comic book superhero, Superman. Superman was followed by other action heroes like Batman and Wonder Woman, the enormous popularity of these heroes led to the next decade being called The Golden Age of Comic Books.

During the 1950s some people called comic books immoral they blamed them for a rise in juvenile delinquency. Some readers may have objected to the content of certain comic strips, the 1950s also saw the appearance of one of the most wholesome and successful comic strips of all time – *Peanuts*. Some comic strips of the 1960s featured political satire one of the most successful of these was *Doonesbury*. Political satire attracts readers it can also be controversial. Some readers have cancelled their newspaper subscriptions after reading an episode of *Doonesbury* some newspapers have refused to publish some of the strip's story lines. So-called "underground" satirical comic strips wanted to distinguish themselves from ordinary comics they called themselves "comix."

Comics like *Peanuts* and *The Simpsons* have made their way onto television, action heroes like Superman and Spider-Man have appeared in enormously successful films. Annual comics conventions draw thousands of visitors comics are even the subject of university classes. Web comics are growing in popularity, they may be the next success story in the long history of comics.

EXERCISE 11C

Part One: Write *two different* corrections for each of the following run-on sentences. (For example, you could make one correction a compound sentence and the other a complex sentence, or you could write two compound sentences with different conjunctions.)

1. The candidate was supposed to win the election he lost by a large margin.

   correction:

   correction:

2. The doctor told him to lose weight he went on a diet.

   correction:

   correction:

3. Our city needs a new library our roads need to be repaired.

   correction:

   correction:

4. The college plans to double student fees some students may have to drop out of school.

   correction:

   correction:

5. John has just lost his job he still plans to take an expensive vacation.

   correction:

   correction:

CORRECTING FRAGMENTS

The basic unit of expression in written English is the sentence. As you already know, *a sentence must contain at least one independent clause.* If you take a group of words that is *not* a complete sentence and punctuate it as though it were a complete sentence, you have created a **sentence fragment.** In other words, you have written only a piece—a fragment—of a sentence rather than a complete sentence.

As you can see. These groups of words. Are fragments.

Because semicolons and periods are usually interchangeable, fragments may also be created by misusing semicolons. If you look carefully at the following two groups of words, you will see that they should form a single complex sentence that needs only a comma, and not a semicolon.

As you can see; wrong punctuation may be confusing.

As you can see, wrong punctuation may be confusing.

Although fragments occur frequently in speech and occasionally in informal writing, they are generally not acceptable in classroom writing and should be avoided in formal writing situations.

There are two types of fragments: **dependent clauses** and **phrases.** As you have already learned in Chapter 10, a dependent clause cannot stand alone as a complete sentence. It must be attached to an independent clause to form a complex sentence.

Therefore, any dependent clause that is separated from its main clause by a period or semicolon is a fragment.

Below are several examples of this type of fragment.

When we arrived at the theater. The movie had already begun.

When we arrived at the theater; the movie had already begun.

We'll miss our plane. If we don't hurry.

We'll miss our plane; if we don't hurry.

Eliminate the dependent clause fragments in the following paragraph by punctuating them correctly.

> Because we are trying to eat more healthful food. We are buying more fruits and vegetables. The problem occurs. Whenever we go to a restaurant. At the restaurant, desserts tempt us; although we have the best of intentions to eat only healthful foods. If we were at home; we would never think of eating pies and ice cream. Because the menu is so intriguing. We wind up ordering things no one would consider to be healthy. When we order banana splits and ice cream; it isn't healthy, but we sure are happy.

Are you remembering to punctuate each dependent clause according to its location? As you learned in Chapter 10, if the *dependent* clause is the first clause in a sentence, it should be followed by a comma. If the *independent* clause is the first clause in a sentence, no comma is needed.

The second type of fragment is the **phrase.** Because a phrase is defined as a group of words that does not contain both a subject and a verb, a phrase obviously cannot be a complete sentence. *All phrases are fragments.* Study the following types of fragments, and notice the way each phrase has been changed from a fragment into a complete sentence.

FRAGMENT—NO SUBJECT   Had seen that film.

SENTENCE   *We* had seen that film.

FRAGMENT—NO VERB	The children on the bus.
SENTENCE	The children *rode* on the bus.
FRAGMENT—INCOMPLETE VERB (-ING FORM)	Kevin attending a conference.
SENTENCE	Kevin *was attending* a conference.

(An -ing main verb must be preceded by a helping verb.)

or

Kevin *attended* a conference.

(Change the -ing verb to a main verb.)

| FRAGMENT—INCOMPLETE VERB (PAST PARTICIPLE) | The garden filled with flowers. |
| SENTENCE | The garden *is filled* with flowers. |

(To be a main verb, a past participle must be preceded by a helping verb. See Chapter 25 for an explanation and a list of past participles.)

FRAGMENT—INFINITIVE	To do well in school.
SENTENCE	*Students must study* hard to do well in school.
FRAGMENT—PARTICIPIAL PHRASE	Being a good friend.
SENTENCE	Being a good friend *takes* a lot of hard work.

The following groups of words are fragments because they lack either a subject or a verb or because they have an incomplete verb. Rewrite each fragment so that it becomes a complete sentence.

The weather being much too cold for swimming.

Ate a pizza for lunch yesterday.

Praying for a good turnout.

The candidate knowing that his lead would not hold.

A present sent by air mail.

The house damaged by the tornado.

The city's new subway system.

When you are writing a composition, be careful not to separate a phrase from the rest of the sentence to which it belongs.

INCORRECT	I'm looking for a small puppy. With floppy white ears.
CORRECT	I'm looking for a small puppy with floppy white ears.
INCORRECT	Wanting to do well; he studied all night.
CORRECT	Wanting to do well, he studied all night.

Rewrite the following items so that any fragments are correctly joined with the sentences to which they belong.

I burned my hand. While frying chicken for dinner.

Pleased with the pianist's performance. The audience demanded an encore.

Susan lay sleeping on the beach. From noon until three o'clock.

To summarize: **Phrases** are sentence fragments because they do not contain both a subject and a complete verb. (In other words, they are not **clauses.**) **Dependent clauses** are fragments because they are not *independent* clauses. This is simply another way of stating the most basic rule of sentence construction:

Every sentence must contain at least one independent clause.

EXERCISE 12A

Correct all of the fragments in the following essay. Some corrections will require attaching dependent clauses or phrases to the independent clauses to which they belong. Other corrections will require adding subjects or verbs. In some cases, a comma should be substituted for a semicolon.

When you were a child. Did your mother pack carrot sticks in your lunch? Carrots being among the most popular vegetables in the United States.

Although carrots are orange now; the original carrots were purple. Yellow and orange carrots did not appear until the sixteenth century. They quickly replaced the older purple carrots. Because purple carrots turned an unappetizing brownish color after being cooked.

Carrots valued by the ancient Greeks and Romans as a love potion. Today scientists encourage the eating of carrots for their nutritional value. A single carrot containing more than the daily requirement of vitamin A for adults. Carrots also good sources of fiber.

Carrots get their orange color from a chemical called carotene. If you eat too many carrots. Your skin can turn yellow. This condition is physically harmless. Although it is visually startling. Dutch farmers in the seventeenth century were aware of this property of carrots. They fed carrots to their cattle. To produce a rich, yellow-colored milk. Housewives borrowed this trick. And added carrot juice to the cream in their churns to turn their butter yellow.

Although it may seem strange. Carrots used to be eaten mainly as desserts. In pies and puddings because of their high sugar content. The English even made carrot jam and carrot wine. Today carrot cake remains a favorite dessert for many people.

Exercise 12B

Correct any fragments that you find in the following essay.

After YouTube was created in February of 2005. The world of the Internet changed. The YouTube website allowing users to upload and share videos with millions of other people. By January, 2008, nearly 70 million users had watched over three billion videos on YouTube.

Before the launch of YouTube in 2005. There were few simple methods available for ordinary computer users to post videos online. With its easy to use interface, YouTube made it possible for anyone with a computer to post a video at the site. Because anyone can upload a video and have millions of people view it within a few minutes. YouTube has made the idea of democracy on the Internet a very real phenomenon. The wide range of topics covered by YouTube making video sharing one of the most important parts of Internet culture.

One of the first major YouTube "hits" was a guitar solo of Pachalbel's canon. Being played by an anonymous young man on an electric guitar. After the video received millions of YouTube views; the *New York Times* revealed the identity of the guitarist as Jeong-Hyun Lim, a twenty-three-year-old from South Korea. In 2009, more than 60 million people watched a YouTube video of Susan Boyle. Performing on a British talent show. This video making Boyle an instant international celebrity. Hoping for the same kind of international discovery. Many musicians and comics and just ordinary people have created their own YouTube videos. However, aspiring performers being only a small percentage of YouTube's videos. YouTube also has videos of concerts by professional musicians, classic film moments and original short films, television clips, and parodies of all sorts.

YouTube even affected the 2008 Presidential election. After a video titled "Obama Girl" became popular on YouTube. Network television stations decided to broadcast it on their own news shows as an example of the growing influence of YouTube. Soon other candidates decided to produce their own YouTube videos. To take advantage of the huge audience of YouTube users. Another example of YouTube's importance occurred when CNN aired a 2008 Presidential primary depbate. Using questions submitted by YouTube users. Because using YouTube allowed a wide range of potential voters to submit questions to their candidates. Many observers believe this was the most democratic of all the Presidential debates.

YouTube has become an enormously successful and powerful new addition to our lives. And an example of how the Internet has made it easy for millions of people to communicate with each other.

EXERCISE 12C

Make each of the following fragments a complete sentence by adding words of your own.

1. Because the earthquake destroyed their home.

   _____

2. The driver making an illegal left turn.

   _____

3. Tired of waiting for the bus.

   _____

4. Wanting to finish college in three years instead of four.

   _____

5. During the last five minutes of the game.

   _____

6. The soldiers sent to Afghanistan.

   _____

7. While waiting for the concert to begin.

   _____

8. The woman hurt in the accident.

   _____

9. If the economy doesn't improve.

   _____

10. The restaurant that was inspected by the health department.

   _____

Unit 3 Review

Part One: 1) Add commas and semicolons (no periods) to the following sentences wherever they are needed. 2) If a sentence does not need any commas or semicolons, label it C for *correct*.

1. Many stores are crowded in December because people are shopping for holiday gifts.

2. Some stores have special sales so that they can attract more customers.

3. If an item is on sale it may sell for as little as half its regular price.

4. Customers can save a lot of money if they shop carefully.

5. Susan Martin needs to be a careful shopper for she has a large family and needs to buy many gifts.

6. Before Susan leaves home she makes a list of places to shop and items to buy.

7. She has a limited amount of money therefore she can't spend too much money on any one person.

8. Her younger children usually get toys the older children get new clothes.

9. Susan buys small gifts for the adults in her large family.

10. The adults have agreed to spend only ten dollars each on gifts for each other so that they can spend more money on the children in their family.

11. It isn't easy to find a ten-dollar gift for an adult so Susan has to spend a lot of time looking for these gifts.

12. On Christmas Day Susan's family will gather at her parents' home so that they can exchange gifts and have a big family dinner.

13. Even though the family members don't give each other a lot of expensive gifts everyone will be very happy.

14. They enjoy celebrating the holiday in addition they enjoy being together.

Part Two: Correct any run-on sentences, comma splices, or fragments that you find in the following essay.

Although many tourists visit Spain. Fewer tourists visit its neighbor, Portugal. Portugal has a lot to offer tourists it has many scenic and historical sites. One of these sites being Cabo da Roca. Cabo da Roca is famous. Because it is the westernmost point in continental Europe. Before the age of explorers. All the land west of Cabo da Roca was unknown territory to most Europeans.

During the sixteenth century, Portugal was a major naval power. Her ships (called caravels) sailed to Africa, Asia, and the Americas. To explore lands then unknown to most Europeans. The first ships to sail completely around the world commanded by a Portuguese navigator. Named Ferdinand Magellan.

The Portuguese are proud of their history as explorers therefore they have made Cabo da Roca a tourist site. You can drive to the government tourist office at Cabo da Roca then you walk several hundred feet to a steep cliff overlooking the sea. A strong wind nearly blows you off your feet such a wind once filled the sails of Portuguese ships bound for the New World. If you have a good imagination. You can almost picture the ships anchored below the cliff.

CHAPTER 13

PARENTHETICAL EXPRESSIONS

When speaking, people often interrupt their sentences with expressions such as *by the way, after all,* or as *a matter of fact.* These expressions are not really part of the main idea of the sentence; instead, they are interrupting—or **parenthetical**—expressions. In speech, people indicate that these parenthetical expressions are not part of the main idea of the sentence by pausing and dropping their voices before and after the expression. In writing, the same pauses are indicated with commas.

You have already learned that commas may be used to separate the clauses in compound and complex sentences. Another major function of the comma is to "set off" interrupting or **parenthetical expressions** from the rest of the sentence in which they occur.

Read the following sentences aloud, and notice how the commas around the italicized parenthetical expressions correspond to the pauses you make in speech.

Well, I guess I have to leave now.

She's only a child, *after all*.

Did you know, *by the way*, that we're getting a new boss?

The rule for punctuating parenthetical expressions is very simple:

A parenthetical expression must be completely set off from the rest of the sentence by commas.

This means that if the parenthetical expression occurs at the *beginning* of the sentence, it is *followed* by a comma. For example,

No, I don't know where they keep their knives.

If the parenthetical expression is at the *end* of the sentence, it is *preceded* by a comma.

The winner of the contest was Judy, *not Jill*.

If the parenthetical expression is in the *middle* of the sentence, it is both *preceded* and *followed* by a comma.

Some seafood, *especially swordfish and tilefish*, may contain harmful amounts of mercury.

There are many parenthetical expressions. Some of the most frequently used ones are listed below:

after all

as a matter of fact

at any rate

etc. (an abbreviation of the Latin words et cetera, meaning "and other things")

for example

for instance

furthermore

however

in fact

nevertheless

of course

on the other hand

on the whole

therefore

well (at the beginning of a sentence)

yes *and* no (at the beginning of a sentence)

Expressions such as the following are often parenthetical if they occur in a position *other than* at the beginning of a sentence:

does it

doesn't it

I believe

I suppose

I hope

I think

is it

isn't it

that is

you know

For example,

He won the election, I believe.

Smoking, you know, is bad for your health.

Continual repetition of the parenthetical expression *you know* should be avoided in both speech and writing. If you are speaking clearly and your listener is paying attention, he or she knows what you are saying and does not have to be constantly reminded of the fact. Besides, you know, continually repeating *you know* can be irritating to your listener, and, you know, it doesn't really accomplish anything.

Study the following points carefully.

1. Some of the above words and phrases can be either parenthetical or not parenthetical, depending on how they are used in a sentence.

If an expression is parenthetical, it can be removed from the sentence, and what remains will still be a complete sentence.

PARENTHETICAL	The problems, *after all*, are difficult.
NOT PARENTHETICAL	He left *after all* the work was done.
PARENTHETICAL	There is a football game today, *I believe*.
NOT PARENTHETICAL	*I believe* what you tell me.

2. Because the abbreviation *etc.* is parenthetical, it must be *preceded* and *followed* by a comma if it occurs in the middle of a sentence.

Books, stationery, art supplies, *etc.*, are sold at the corner store.

The final comma after *etc.* indicates that *etc.* is parenthetical. Notice that this comma serves a different function from the commas that separate the items in the series.

3. **Conjunctive adverbs,** like *however* and *nevertheless*, are considered parenthetical and are set off from the clause in which they occur. They should be punctuated in simple sentences as follows:

I thought the plan was a secret. *However*, everyone seems to know about it.

or

I thought the plan was a secret. Everyone, *however*, seems to know about it.

In the second clause of a compound sentence, **conjunctive adverbs** should be punctuated as follows:

She earns a good salary; *nevertheless*, she always seems to be borrowing money from her friends.

The concert was long; *however*, it was quite beautiful.

The semicolon is needed because the clauses in the compound sentence are not joined by a coordinating conjunction. The semicolon also takes the place of the comma that would normally precede a parenthetical expression occurring in the middle of a sentence. A comma follows the parenthetical expression to set it off from the remainder of the sentence.

4. People's names and titles are also set off by commas *if you are speaking directly to them* in a sentence. This type of construction is called **direct address.** The punctuation of direct address is the same as that used for parenthetical expressions.

Have you played your guitar today, *Allen?*

Ladies and gentlemen, please be seated.

Notice that names and titles are set off by commas only when the person is being *directly addressed* in the sentence. Otherwise, no commas are needed.

Music has always been important to Allen. (no commas)

Allen, have you always loved music? (comma for direct address)

Exercise 13A

Add commas and semicolons to the following sentences wherever they are needed. If a sentence needs no additional punctuation, label it *C* for *correct*. This exercise deals only with the punctuation rules in Chapter 13.

1. All of us know that we need a good night's sleep don't we?

2. However many Americans do not get the sleep they need.

3. On the whole doctors believe that adults need about eight hours of sleep each night.

4. Nevertheless many Americans sleep for only five or six hours.

5. Lack of sleep has negative effects on our health in fact it can contribute to several serious diseases.

6. The most immediate effect of sleep loss is an inability to concentrate for example sleep-deprived students may have more trouble answering test items correctly.

7. Habitual lack of sleep can contribute to weight gain therefore if people want to lose weight, they should be sure to get a good night's sleep.

8. Lack of sleep has been linked to diabetes furthermore it seems to increase a person's chances of developing high-blood pressure and heart problems.

9. Teenagers need even more sleep than adults in fact they should get nine hours of sleep each night.

10. Of course few teenagers are able to sleep that long because of their busy schedules with school, work, social activities etc.

11. Teenagers not only need more sleep than adults in addition research shows that they have more trouble waking up early in the morning than adults do.

12. Some schools are aware of this problem therefore they now begin the school day around nine o'clock instead of at eight.

13. Certain conditions of modern life contribute to sleep deprivation for example time spent commuting.

14. Homes in outlying areas are often cheaper than homes in a city thus many workers spend long hours commuting to and from their jobs.

15. In areas like Southern California for instance commuters often drive more than a hundred miles each day.

16. Furthermore these drivers may leave home before five in the morning in order to avoid rush-hour traffic.

17. Of course leaving home early in the morning and arriving home from work late in the evening leaves less time for sleeping.

18. In addition sleepy drivers are a danger on the road.

19. Working mothers are often sleep-deprived in fact they may get even fewer hours of sleep than their husbands.

20. Their work day does not end when their office closes after all they have a whole new set of tasks waiting for them at home.

21. Well someone must prepare dinner, do laundry, and take care of the children.

22. That person is usually the mother in the family isn't it?

23. I suppose that many of us try to adjust our schedules so that we can get more sleep.

24. However I still notice a lot of sleepy people around me each day.

EXERCISE 13B

Add commas and semicolons to the following essay wherever they are necessary. This exercise requires adding punctuation only for parenthetical expressions.

I know most people love roller coasters; However I'm not one of those. Roller coasters have always scared me. As a matter of fact I can't even look at a roller coaster without feeling sick! Nevertheless I have found that sometimes knowledge helps me to feel less fear. Well I am determined to learn a little about roller coasters!

The name "roller coaster" has two possible origins. I believe that it may have come from an early American design of a sled fitted with rollers that coasted over a slide or ramp. On the other hand some people think it came from a ride at a Massachusetts roller skating rink in 1887. What is certain at any rate is the patent of the first roller coaster in 1885 by LaMarcus Adna Thompson. He created a specialized railroad system that had a track that rose and fell in patterns. You know it's those up and down and loops and riding upside down motions that some people love about roller coasters; However I find this patented design terrifying!

The first patent may have occurred in the nineteenth century; however roller coasters were around as long ago as the 1700s. The oldest roller coasters I believe go back to what were called Russian Mountains. As a matter of fact they were not mountains; they were hills made of ice and were located around St. Petersburg, Russia. They were I think pretty scary because they were as high as 80 feet and had a 50 degree drop and no seatbelts! In many countries today in fact roller coasters are still called Russian Mountains.

At any rate LaMarcus Adna Thompson is the father of the roller coaster for Americans. Yes he is the one I blame for bringing this ride into all of our lives. His patent was based on a mining company's design in 1827 for a gravity railroad. The company used this railroad to deliver coal however by the 1850s, the Gravity Road had become a ride for thrill-seekers. Mr. Thompson's genius I suppose was to introduce this gravity design to Coney Island in New York. In fact he created dark tunnels with painted scenery that became standard in amusement parks all across the country. Coney Island is better known however for the Cyclone, a terrifying roller coaster that opened in 1927.

Historians see the Great Depression as the end of this first Golden Age of roller coasters. These were all wooden roller coasters. Disney of course created a whole new design that changed roller coasters. In 1959, Disneyland introduced the Matterhorn Bobsleds. What makes this ride different is its use of a tubular steel track. This new design allows for the kinds of movements that I hate. Unlike the wooden railroad ties, tubular steel can bend in any direction for example incorporating loops, corkscrews and other scary moves! The second Golden Age began in 1972 with the building of the *The* Racer at Kings Island in Ohio. In addition new designs and technologies like electromagnetically launched coasters have I think made roller coaster rides even more exciting.

You know statistically roller coasters are very safe. The Consumer Product Safety Commission has estimated only about two fatalities a year related to amusement parks. Such facts can make a person feel all right about these rides I suppose. Well I can't be satisfied. No I believe there isn't enough statistical assurance in the entire universe to get me on something like for example Six Flags' Goliath or Batman the Ride or even baby roller coasters!

On the other hand, if a phrase is necessary to establish the specific identity of a noun, it is *not set off* by commas. Study the difference between the following two sentences.

The novel *Great Expectations* is considered by many critics to be Charles Dickens's greatest work. (No commas are used to set off *Great Expectations* because the title is necessary to identify which of Dickens's many novels is considered to be his greatest work.)

Charles Dickens's fourteenth novel, *Great Expectations,* is considered by many critics to be his greatest work. (Commas are used to set off *Great Expectations* because Dickens's greatest work has already been specifically identified as his *fourteenth* novel.)

Most single-word appositives are necessary to establish the specific identity of the nouns they follow and are, therefore, *not* set off by commas.

The color *yellow* is my favorite.

My sister *Susan* lives in Detroit.

The word *penurious* means "stingy."

Underline the appositives in the following sentences, and then add commas wherever they are necessary. Some sentences may not require commas.

Fiat automobiles are manufactured in Turin a city in northeastern Italy.

The komodor a Hungarian sheepdog has a coat that looks like a mop.

Balboa a sixteenth-century Spanish explorer was the first European to discover the American side of the Pacific Ocean.

In Europe, fruits and vegetables are usually sold by the kilogram an amount equal to 2.2 pounds.

Joan's husband an orthopedic surgeon spends much of his time working on injured athletes.

Have you seen the movie *Titanic?*

EXERCISE 14A

Add commas to the following sentences wherever they are necessary. This exercise covers only the rules from Chapter 14.

1. Have you heard of Jim Thorpe the most famous athlete of the early twentieth century?

2. Jim Thorpe (1887–1953) was an American Indian a member of the Sauk and Fox tribe.

3. At the age of seven, Thorpe was sent to a boarding school for Native Americans the Carlisle Industrial Indian School in Pennyslvania.

4. As its name suggests, the school prepared its students for careers working with their hands the kind of jobs believed appropriate at the time for Native Americans.

5. Thorpe began his athletic career at Carlisle by participating in two sports football and track.

6. His football coach at Carlisle was the legendary Glenn "Pop" Warner the founder of the Pop Warner Youth Football League.

7. In 1909 and 1910, Thorpe won his first national athletic awards membership on the All-American football team for both years.

8. In 1912, Thorpe became a member of the American track and field team for the 1912 Olympics and won gold medals in the two most difficult track and field events the pentathlon and the decathlon.

9. However, the next year 1913 the International Olympic Committee began proceedings that eventually stripped Thorpe of his medals.

10. Because Thorpe had played semi-professional baseball for two seasons after graduating from Carlisle, he was considered a professional athlete a person ineligible for Olympic competition.

11. After the Olympics, Thorpe returned to the sport that had caused him to lose his gold medals professional baseball and played for twenty years.

12. In his last baseball season the best season of his entire career Thorpe batted .327 in sixty games for the Boston Braves.

13. Record books record Thorpe's most amazing baseball feat hitting three home runs into three different states in a single game.

14. During a game in a ballpark on the Texas-Oklahoma-Arkansas border, Thorpe hit a ball over the left-field wall his first home run of the game.

15. His second homer went over the right-field wall into Arkansas, and his third homer an inside-the-ballpark home run was hit into center field in Texas.

16. During many of his baseball years, Thorpe was also a star football player and helped to organize the American Professional Football Association the forerunner of the National Football League.

17. Thorpe is also remembered for his most amazing football play kicking a wind-assisted punt of ninety-five yards from his own five-yard line.

18. In 1950, the nation's press corps not only selected Thorpe as the best football player of the first half of the twentieth century but also gave him an even greater honor best athlete of the half-century.

19. The one black mark on Thorpe's career the loss of his 1912 gold medals was erased when the International Olympic Committee reversed its decision and returned Thorpe's gold medals to his family in 1983.

20. In 2000 Jim Thorpe received his highest honor selection as the best athlete of the entire twentieth century by viewers of ABC's *Wide World of Sports*.

Exercise 14B

Add commas and semicolons to the following essay wherever they are needed. This exercise covers the punctuation of both appositives and parenthetical expressions.

Most people I think have heard of Bill Gates the founder of Microsoft. His biography after all is very interesting. Along with his partner Paul Allen, Bill Gates is probably one of the most recognized entrepreneurs of the personal computer revolution. He is also the author of two books, *The Road Ahead* and *Business & the Speed of Thought*. In addition he is incredibly wealthy. He is, in fact, the third richest person in the world after having been the richest person in the world for fifteen years in a row! In 2000, Bill Gates stepped down as chief executive officer of Microsoft, but he remained its chairman and created a new position for himself chief software architect. Gates has also become respected for his charitable efforts. The Bill & Melinda Gates Foundation, a charitable and scientific enterprise was established in 2000 and is a major philanthropic endeavor. In fact in 2006, Gates resigned to work full-time for his charities.

Born in Seattle, Washington, Bill Gates came from a wealthy family. His father, a prominent lawyer, his mother, a member of the board of directors of United Way, were both well-known people. They provided Bill with opportunities few of us can imagine. His interest in computers began when he was quite young and a student at the Lakeside School an exclusive preparatory school. When he was in the eighth grade, the school's Mother's Club bought the school computer time on a General Electric computer. Gates a thirteen-year-old adolescent became fascinated with programming. He learned how to use the current program BASIC and figured out how to create a tic-tac-toe game for his friends to play against the computer. He and Paul Allen his long-time friend got into trouble one summer exploiting bugs on Computer Center Corporation's operating system so that they could get free computer time!

Of course Bill Gates was an extremely intelligent student. Everyone has heard of his high SAT score 1590 out of 1600 and his probable IQ of 170 a one in a million level. After graduating from the Lakeside School in 1973, he went to Harvard. At Harvard, Gates found computers more interesting than his classes. After discussing his plans with his parents, Gates dropped out of Harvard and began his own company with Paul Allen his childhood friend.

The rest I think has been a story of an entrepreneurial genius. Gates the inventor and businessman created Microsoft one of the most successful companies the world has seen and its principal product Windows. During his active years with the company from 1975 to 2006 Gates was primarily responsible for key company issues for example its product strategy. Some aspects of his management style for example his combative nature and harsh straight talk have been criticized by his peers. Nevertheless he is still one of the world's most successful and influential people.

Nonrestrictive clauses must be completely set off from the rest of the sentence by commas.

This means that if a nonrestrictive clause is at the *end* of a sentence, it will be *preceded* by a comma. If it is in the *middle* of a sentence, it will be *both preceded and followed* by a comma. (Like appositives, nonrestrictive clauses never occur at the beginning of a sentence because they must follow the noun that they describe.)

The restrictive and nonrestrictive clauses that you have been studying are called adjective clauses because, like adjectives, these clauses describe nouns. The words that most frequently introduce adjective clauses are:

that

where

which

who

whom

whose

Like all clauses, adjective clauses must contain both a subject and a verb. But notice that in adjective clauses *the word that introduces the clause may also be the subject of the clause.*

S   V

The house *that once occupied this lot* was destroyed by fire.

Or the clause may contain a separate subject:

S V

The wallet *that I lost* contained all my credit cards.

Adjective clauses, like adverb clauses, are used in **complex sentences.** Although these sentences may not seem to be complex at first glance, if you study the sentences above, you will see that each of them has two subjects and two verbs. Also, if the adjective clause, which is the **dependent clause,** is removed from the sentence, a complete independent clause remains.

S   V

INDEPENDENT CLAUSE   The house was destroyed by fire.

S   V

DEPENDENT CLAUSE   that once occupied this lot

	S V
INDEPENDENT CLAUSE	The wallet contained all my credit cards.

	S V
DEPENDENT CLAUSE	that I lost

An adjective clause often occurs in the middle of a sentence because it must follow the noun it describes. When an adjective clause is in the middle of a sentence, part of the independent clause precedes it, and the rest of the independent clause follows it. For example,

S   V

Food *that is high in calories* often tastes better than low-calorie food.

S   V

The National Museum of the American Indian, which used to be located in New York City, is now in Washington, D.C.

A sentence may contain more than one adjective clause. Each clause is punctuated separately. In the following sentences, the first adjective clause is *nonrestrictive* (with commas), and the second clause is *restrictive* (no commas).

The San Fernando Valley, *which suffered a large earthquake in 1994*, has since experienced aftershocks *that distress many people.*

The Cadillac automobile, *which was originally manufactured in Detroit*, is named after the French explorer *who founded the city.*

Underline every adjective clause in each of the following sentences, and circle the noun it describes. Then decide which clauses are restrictive (and do *not* need commas) and which clauses are nonrestrictive (and *do* need commas). Add the appropriate punctuation.

Note: Although clauses beginning with *who, whom, whose,* or *where* may be either restrictive or nonrestrictive, clauses that begin with *that* are *always* restrictive. In addition, many writers prefer to use *which* only for nonrestrictive clauses.

Union Square which is one of San Francisco's main shopping areas is known for its open-air flower stalls.

The classes that I am taking this semester are all easy for me.

Most tourists who come to Los Angeles also visit Disneyland which is less than an hour's drive from the city.

The candidate whom we supported was not elected.

Ms. Gomez whose native language is Spanish also speaks French, German, and English.

He is an artist whom we all admire a great deal.

EXERCISE 15A

Each of the following sentences contains one or more adjective clauses. Underline each adjective clause, and circle the noun it describes. If the clause is nonrestrictive and needs additional punctuation, add commas wherever they are needed. If all of the adjective clauses in a sentence are restrictive and the sentence needs no additional punctuation, label it *C* for *correct*.

1. Sometimes an author who was world-famous a generation or two ago can be rediscovered by today's readers.

2. This happened to Pearl Buck who was the first American woman to win the Nobel Prize for literature.

3. Buck's most famous novel is *The Good Earth* which describes the life of a farmer in a Chinese village.

4. Pearl Buck was born in West Virginia in 1892, but she spent most of the first forty years of her life in China where her parents were Presbyterian missionaries.

5. Because her parents hired a Chinese scholar to give her lessons in the language and culture of China, Buck knew much more about China than most of the foreigners who lived there.

6. In 1910, Buck returned to the United States to attend Randolph-Macon Woman's College which was located in Virginia.

7. After finishing college and returning to China, Buck married a man who was an agricultural economist.

8. John Buck's job was to teach traditional Chinese farmers modern agricultural techniques that would improve their productivity.

9. During the years she spent with her first husband, Buck gathered material about rural life in China that she would use in many of her later novels.

10. During the 1920s, Buck began to write stories and essays that were published in leading American magazines, like the *Nation* and the *Atlantic Monthly*.

11. In 1930, the John Day Company published her first novel, *East Wind, West Wind* which told the story of a traditional Chinese woman who learns about Western civilization when she marries a doctor who was educated in the United States.

12. Richard Walsh who worked at John Day would later become Buck's second husband.

13. Buck's second novel, *The Good Earth* which established her reputation as a writer became the best-selling novel of both 1931 and 1932.

14. It won the 1932 Pulitzer Prize which is awarded each year for the best American works of literature.

15. *The Good Earth* is the story of a Chinese farmer named Wang Lung who begins his adult life as a small village farmer but eventually becomes a wealthy landowner.

16. Buck became even more famous when *The Good Earth* was made into a movie that appeared in 1937.

17. Because of Hollywood's racial policies at the time, the leading roles of Wang Lung and his wife O-Lan were played by actors who were European.

18. They wore make-up that made them look somewhat Asian.

19. Luise Rainer who played the role of O-Lan studied the behavior of a real Chinese woman who had been hired as an extra on the set.

20. Rainer's attempts to act like a Chinese peasant woman impressed Buck who watched part of the filming.

21. Buck's high opinion of Ranier's acting was shared by the Motion Picture Academy which gave Ranier an Oscar for best actress in 1937.

22. In 1938, Buck was given the Nobel Prize which is the highest award that an author can receive.

23. As years passed, Buck fell out of fashion with readers who preferred to read Chinese authors writing about their own country.

24. However, *The Good Earth* remained in print and was read by many students whose first knowledge of Chinese life came from reading this novel in their English classes.

25. Then 2004 saw an event that put *The Good Earth* back on the best-seller list for the first time since 1932.

26. The novel came to the attention of Oprah Winfrey who made it a selection of her book club.

27. Viewers who watched Oprah's television show heard about the book and rushed out to buy it.

28. It is appropriate for a woman who is one of television's most important personalities to honor the first American woman to win both the Pulitzer and the Nobel prizes.

EXERCISE 15B

Add commas and semicolons to the following sentences wherever they are necessary. This exercise covers the punctuation of parenthetical expressions, appositives, and restrictive and nonrestrictive clauses. If a sentence needs no additional punctuation, mark it C for *correct*.

1. The Internet has spawned social networking sites that have changed the lives of millions of people.

2. One of these is Twitter a social networking and micro-blogging site founded in 2006.

3. Twitter can be accessed in a number of ways that include mobile phones, a logged-in home page, and m.twitter.com.

4. Twitter gets its name from something called a "tweet" a message not more than 140 characters or less.

5. Because of its tweets, Twitter has an immediacy that is fun and engaging.

6. The heart of Twitter is one question "What are you doing?"

7. Some people leave a trail of their daily experiences that can range from such activities as "I'm brushing my teeth" to "I just took a test" to "I'm listening to my favorite Metallica song."

8. You can learn about your friends' activities by simply clicking on the site's "followers" link which allows you to receive all these tweets.

9. You may learn for instance that a friend loves growing carrots or watching basketball.

10. Each page has the layout of a blog a personal website that functions as an online journal.

11. Since it was created in 2006, Twitter which now has 5 million users has become one of the Internet's most popuar sites.

12. Twitter began as a research and development project inside Odeo a San Francisco podcasting company that initially used Twitter for its own employees.

13. Just a few months after its creation, Twitter became a product of a new company Obvious which watched the product increase in popularity with other Internet users.

14. Its three founders Jack Dorsey, Biz Stone, and Evan Williams accepted the South by Southwest Web Award in the blog category in 2007.

15. Dorsey the man behind Twitter accepted the award by joking, "We'd like to thank you in 140 characters or less. And we just did!"

16. Because the Internet has such far-reaching influence, Twitter has been translated into languages that range from Arabic to Hindi to Hebrew to Afrikaans to French.

17. Twitter is used mainly by people who want to know about their friends' daily activities.

18. Twitter however has been also discovered by a variety of different businesses and entities that are interested in providing products or service information.

19. Cisco Systems, Jet Blue, and Whole Foods Markets are some of the businesses that use Twitter to have regular communication with clients or customers.

20. NASA the National Aeronautics and Space Administration has used Twitter to provide updates on its Space Shuttle missions and on other space programs that interest the public.

21. Some universities even use Twitter to communicate information to those students who pay more attention to . . . their Twitter site than to other forms of communication.

22. Incredibly, 10 Downing Street the website of the British Prime Minister has also started using Twitter.

23. Many news outlets that include the BBC, CNC, CNN and MSNBC use Twitter to disseminate breaking news and to create a relationship with their viewers.

24. Not surprisingly, technology-savvy President Obama used Twitter during his election campaign in ways that some people believe helped him to win over the youth vote.

25. Twitter is a website that gives people a window into the daily lives of their friends.

26. Similar to reality television shows, Twitter uses our cell phones and computers to create worlds that we can share with one another.

EXERCISE 15C

Part One: Write your own complex sentences using the words listed below to form *restrictive* clauses. Underline the adjective clauses in each of your sentences, and circle the word the clause describes.

Example: where

Have you ever visited the Circle the word City <u>where your parents were born?</u>

1. that:

2. who:

3. whose:

4. where:

Part Two: Write your own complex sentences using the words listed below to form *nonrestrictive* clauses. Underline the adjective clause in each of your sentences, and circle the noun that the clause describes. Add commas wherever they are needed.

5. who:

6. which:

7. whose:

8. where:

C H A P T E R

Commas with Introductory Phrases, Series, Dates, and Addresses

Introductory Phrases

In Chapter 10 you learned to put a comma after an introductory dependent clause (a dependent clause at the beginning of a sentence). It is also customary to place a comma after other types of material at the beginning of a sentence to separate the introductory information from the clause that follows it:

a prepositional phrase, or a combination of prepositional phrases, that is four words or longer

> *At exactly 9 A.M. on the first Monday of every month,* the president of the company meets with her board of directors.

an introductory phrase beginning with a present participle (an *–ing* form of a verb)

> *Hurrying to catch her cab,* Marlene tripped and sprained her ankle.
>
> *Hoping to get something to eat,* the homeless family headed for the nearest food bank.

175

an introductory phrase beginning with a past participle (an *–ed* form of a verb)

Frightened by the noise, the baby woke up and began to cry.
Covered in flames, the home quickly burned to the ground.

A SERIES OF ITEMS

A series consists of *three* or *more* related items. Commas are placed between each item in a series.

Danish, Swedish, and *Norwegian* are related languages.

For dessert you may choose *ice cream, sherbet,* or *tapioca.*

To qualify for this job, you must *have a master's degree in international relations, at least three years of work experience, and the ability to speak both Spanish and Portuguese.*

Although some writers consider the final comma before the conjunction (*and, or,* or *nor*) optional, using it is preferred, especially in formal writing.

However, if *every* item in a series is joined by a conjunction, no commas are needed because the conjunctions keep the individual items separated. This type of construction is used only when the writer wishes to place particular emphasis on the number of items in the series.

The backyard of this house has a *swimming pool* and *a Jacuzzi* and *a hot tub.*

DATES AND ADDRESSES

If a date or an address consists of more than one item, a comma is used after *each* part of the date or the address, *including a comma after the last item.* (If the last item in the series is also the last word in the sentence, only a period follows it.) Notice that this punctuation rule differs from the rule used for punctuating an ordinary series.

My grandparents will celebrate their fiftieth wedding anniversary on October 11, 2009, with a party for all of their family.

The name of the month and the number of the day (October 11) are considered a single item and are separated from the year by a comma. However, notice that a comma also *follows* 1999, which is the last item in the date.

We moved from Norman, Oklahoma, to Flagstaff, Arizona, in 1995.

Notice the commas after "Oklahoma" and "Arizona." These commas are used in addition to the commas that separate the names of the cities from the names of the states.

If a date or an address consists of only a single item, no comma is necessary.

December 25 is Christmas.

We moved from Oklahoma to Arizona.

A comma is not used before a ZIP code number.

The mailing address for Hollywood is Los Angeles, California 90028.

Punctuate the following sentences.

The armistice signed on November 11, 1918 ended the fighting in World War I.

Because of the multicultural character of my neighborhood, church bazaars sell tacos pizza teriyaki chow mein and hot dogs.

The coffee shop's special club sandwich contains ham and cheese and turkey.

I can't believe that you drove from Portland Oregon to Newark New Jersey in three days.

John F. Kennedy Aldous Huxley and C. S. Lewis all died on November 22 1963.

EXERCISE 16A

Add commas to the following sentences wherever they are needed. If a sentence needs no additional punctuation, label it *C* for *correct*. This exercise covers the punctuation of introductory phrases, items in a series, and dates and addresses.

1. From Monday June 7 through Sunday June 13 the Carpenter family will be in Orlando Florida.

2. Originally, the family had planned to visit only one or two theme parks; however, the Carpenter children persuaded their parents to go to Walt Disney World and SeaWorld and Universal Studios!

3. Excited by their upcoming vacation the children are already planning which rides to take and which exhibits to see at the various theme parks.

4. They are looking at computer web sites reading travel brochures and listening to suggestions from their friends.

5. Hoping to save some money the children's parents have decided to stay at the Holiday Inn in Orlando.

6. The Holiday Inn offers a discount for Automobile Club members free shuttle rides to SeaWorld and Universal Studios and a kitchenette for preparing meals.

7. The address of the inn is 5905 Kirkman Road Orlando Florida 32819.

8. The family plans to drive to Orlando from their home in Baltimore Maryland instead of flying.

9. On their way to Florida they will stop to tour a college in Virginia to look at furniture outlets in North Carolina and to visit relatives in Georgia.

10. The family hopes that this vacation will give them a chance to see new places to have lots of fun together and to create many happy memories for the future.

11. During much of 2008 and 2009 the United States was in an economic recession.

12. On May 16 2009 the Associated Press published an article about products that were selling well despite the recession.

13. The Hormel Foods Corporation reported increased sales of Dinty Moore stew canned chili and Spam.

14. All of these products provide meals that are inexpensive filling and easy to prepare.

15. For very similar reasons Kraft Foods reported a double-digit growth in the sale of macaroni and cheese.

16. Stressed by the difficult economic conditions consumers also bought more over-the-counter medicines.

17. Sales increased for headache remedies antacids and laxatives.

18. According to the Burpee Seed Company more people are buying fruit and vegetable seeds.

19. Sales of its tomato and lettuce and green-bean seeds have increased by thirty percent.

20. In fact, the company started a basic-training course called a "root camp" at its headquarters at 300 Park Avenue Warminster Pennsylvania 18974.

EXERCISE 16C

After you write the following sentences, reread them to make certain that they are punctuated correctly.

1. Write a sentence containing an address. The address you use should need at least two commas.

2. Write a sentence containing a date. The date you use should need at least two commas.

3. Write a sentence that contains a series of three items, with the conjunction *and* joining two of the items.

4. Write a sentence that contains a series of three items, with the conjunction *or* joining two of the items.

5. Write a sentence in which *every* item in the series is joined by *and* or *or.*

6. Write a sentence beginning with a prepositional phrase. The prepositional phrase you use should contain at least four words.

7. Write a sentence beginning with a phrase that starts with a present participle.

8. Write a sentence beginning with a phrase that starts with a past participle.

UNIT 4 REVIEW

Add commas and semicolons to the following essay wherever they are necessary. This exercise covers the punctuation of parenthetical expressions, direct-address, appositives, restrictive and nonrestrictive clauses, introductory phrases, series, dates, and addresses.

The 1939 Academy Awards were presented on February 29 1940 in Los Angeles California. Nineteen thirty-nine was an exceptional year for movies in fact film critics have labeled it "the greatest year in film history." Furthermore members of the Academy of Motion Picture Arts and Sciences had a very large number of films to consider. Today only five films are nominated for the year's best picture however ten films were nominees for the honor of "outstanding production" of the year 1939.

Although all ten films that were nominated that year are excellent movies, the two best-known of these films *The Wizard of Oz* and *Gone with the Wind* remained popular for decades because they were often broadcast on television. You have seen at least one of these films haven't you? It's a coincidence isn't it that both of these films were based on best-selling novels. The novel *The Wizard of Oz* is a children's story that was published in 1900. Its author L. Frank Baum created a fantasy about a young girl who is transported from a farm in Kansas to the magical Land of Oz. Baum got the name for his magical kingdom when he glanced at a file cabinet drawer that contained files from O–Z. Even people who have never seen the movie are familiar with the song "Over the Rainbow" which was sung by Judy Garland who played the lead role of Dorothy in the film.

The movie *Gone with the Wind* closely follows the plot of the novel that inspired it. Margaret Mitchell's *Gone with the Wind* which won the Pulitzer Prize for 1937 tells the story of the Civil War from the Southern point of view. Its main character Scarlett O'Hara struggles to keep her family's plantation going as the South gradually loses the war. Vivien Leigh the English actress portraying Scarlett in the film won an Oscar as the best actress of 1939. An Oscar for best supporting actress was won by Hattie McDaniel who played the role of Scarlett's nursemaid and became the first African American performer to win an Oscar. However although Leigh's leading man in the film Clark Gable was nominated for the Best Actor award, he lost to Robert Donat the actor playing the role of an English private-school teacher in the film *Goodbye, Mr. Chips*.

Goodbye, Mr. Chips by the way was also based on a best-selling novel, as were *Wuthering Heights* and *Of Mice and Men* two of the other nominated films. Three other nominated films featured famous actresses in romantic roles. Bette Davis the star of *Dark Victory* plays the role of a wealthy woman who falls in love with the doctor treating her for a terminal brain tumor. *Ninotchka* which starred the famous Greta Garbo is a romantic comedy about a Russian spy who is sent on a secret mission to Paris where she falls in love with a French count. Irene Dunne starred in a movie whose theme is obvious from its title *Love Affair*. This film inspired two remakes the 1957 *An*

SUBJECT, OBJECT, AND POSSESSIVE PRONOUNS

Pronouns are words that are used to refer to persons, places, things, and ideas without repeating their names. In other words, pronouns are used in place of nouns. For example, rather than saying "Ben lost Ben's notebook last night, but Ben found the notebook this morning," you can say, "Ben lost *his* notebook last night, but *he* found *it* this morning." In this sentence, the pronoun *his* replaces Ben's, the pronoun *he* replaces Ben, and the pronoun *it* replaces notebook. The noun that the pronoun replaces is called the **antecedent** (Latin for "to go before") of the pronoun.

There are several different kinds of pronouns, but in this chapter you will be studying only **subject pronouns, object pronouns,** and **possessive pronouns.**

Singular Pronouns

Subject	Object	Possessive
I	me	my, mine
you	you	your, yours
he	him	his
she	her	her, hers
it	it	its

Plural Pronouns

Subject	Object	Possessive
we	us	our, ours
you	you	your, yours
they	them	their, theirs

As their name suggests, **subject pronouns** are used as the subject of a sentence or a clause. For example,

He is a good dancer.

We went to the park together.

In *formal* speech and writing, subject pronouns are also used after forms of the verb *be,* as in:

That is *she* singing with the chorus.

It is *I* who need your help.

If I were *she,* I'd have come to the lecture.

In formal speech and writing, subject pronouns are used after forms of the verb *be* because they refer to the *same* thing or person as the subject.

That = she singing with the chorus.

It = I.

I = *she.*

However, in *informal* speech, many people would use object pronouns in the sentences below.

That is (or That's) *her* singing with the chorus.

It is (or It's) *me*.

If I were *her*, I'd have come to the lecture.

Whether you choose to say "it is I" or "it is me" depends on the circumstances. If you are taking an English test or writing a formal essay, using subject pronouns after forms of *be* is appropriate and expected. But if you are speaking casually with a friend, "It is I" may sound artificial, and the informal "It is me" might be more suitable.

In this unit, you will be studying both grammar and usage. Try to keep clear in your mind those situations in which you have a choice between formal and informal constructions (usage) and those situations in which only one pronoun form is correct at all times (grammar).

"It is *we*" versus "It is *us*" = usage.

"Al and *I* are here" versus "Al and *me* are here" = grammar.

Object pronouns are used as objects of prepositions, as direct objects, and as indirect objects.

You will remember that the noun or pronoun in a prepositional phrase is called **the object of the preposition.** That is why an object pronoun replaces the noun. For example,

The award was given to *Matthew*.

The award was given to *him*.

Please sit by *Cathy*.

Please sit by *her*.

Object pronouns are also used as direct objects. A **direct object** is the word that *receives* the action of the verb and, with very few exceptions, follows the verb, often as the next word.

<pre>
     S   DO
</pre>
The artist painted that *picture*.

The artist painted *it*.

<pre>
  S   DO
</pre>
He composed that *song* last night.

He composed *it* last night.

Another way that object pronouns are used is as indirect objects. An **indirect object** is the person or thing *to whom or for whom* something is done.

S   IO   DO

She made *Robert* a chocolate cake.

She made *him* a chocolate cake.

The preceding sentence is another way of saying, "She made a chocolate cake *for him.*"

S   IO   DO

Benjamin gave his sister a gift.

Benjamin gave *her* a gift.

The preceding sentence is another way of saying, "Benjamin gave a gift to *her.*" **Possessive pronouns** are used to show ownership.

The cat scratched *its* neck.

The children stamped *their* feet in joy.

Very few people make pronoun errors when there is only one subject or one object in a sentence. For example, no native speaker of English would say, "Us is here" instead of "We are here." However, people often do make mistakes when two subjects or two objects are paired up in a sentence. For example, which of the following two sentences is grammatically correct?

Barbara bought Kevin and *me* some good cookies.

Barbara bought Kevin and *I* some good cookies.

To determine the correct pronoun in this kind of "double" construction, split the sentence in two like this:

1. Barbara bought Kevin some good cookies.
2. Barbara bought (me, I) some good cookies.

As you can tell after you have split the sentence in two, it would be incorrect to say, "Barbara bought *I* some good cookies." The correct pronoun is *me,* which is the indirect object of the verb *bought.* Therefore, the whole sentence should read:

Barbara bought Kevin and me some good cookies.

Which of the following two sentences is correct?

The mayor congratulated Rick and *I*.

The mayor congratulated Rick and *me*.

Again, split the sentences in two.

1. The mayor congratulated Rick.
2. The mayor congratulated (me, I).

Now, which pronoun is correct?

Another very common pronoun error is using subject pronouns instead of object pronouns after prepositions. The object of a preposition must be an *object pronoun*. Which of the following two sentences is correct?

The teacher handed new books to Sam and *I*.

The teacher handed new books to Sam and *me*.

If you split the sentence in two, you have:

1. The teacher handed new books to Sam.
2. The teacher handed new books to (me, I).

The correct pronoun is *me*, which is the object of the preposition *to*. Therefore, the correct sentence is:

The teacher handed new books to Sam and *me*.

It is extremely important that you do not decide which pronoun to use simply on the basis of what "sounds better" *unless you split the sentence in two first*. To many people, "The teacher handed new books to Sam and *I*" sounds "more correct" than "The teacher handed new books to Sam and *me*," yet, as you have seen, *me* is actually the correct pronoun.

Another example of choosing an incorrect pronoun because it "sounds better" is the frequent misuse of the subject pronoun *I* after the preposition *between*. As you already know, the object of a preposition must be an *object* pronoun. Therefore, it is always incorrect to say "between you and *I*." The correct construction is "between you and *me*."

Circle the pronoun that correctly completes each of the following sentences.

Between you and (I, me), that's a wonderful movie.

The teacher rewarded Joseph and (I, me) for our presentation.

Ken and (she, her) speak frequently.

Helene made Sasha and (I, me) Halloween costumes.

The party was for their class and (we, us).

Occasionally you may use constructions like the following:

We freshmen must pre-enroll for our classes.

Most of *us nurses* would prefer to work the 7 A.M. to 3 P.M. shift.

To determine whether the sentence requires a subject or an object pronoun, see which pronoun would be correct if the pronoun appeared in the sentence by itself rather than being followed by a noun.

(We, us) citizens should vote in each election.

(We, us) should vote in each election.

Give a raise to (we, us) good workers.

Give a raise to (we, us).

The correct pronouns are *we* citizens and *us* workers.

Circle the pronoun that correctly completes each of the following sentences.

Some theaters give a discount to (we, us) students.

Actors depend on the support of (we, us) fans.

(We, us) customers want the store to stay open later.

EXERCISE 17A

The first part of this exercise is intended as a quick review of subject and object pronouns. Reverse each sentence so that the subject pronoun becomes the object and the object pronoun becomes the subject.

> Example: *I* helped *him* complete the report.
> Answer: *He* helped *me* complete the report.

1. *You* should phone *us* tonight.

2. *They* have known *me* for years.

3. *She* hired *him* three months ago.

4. *We* invited *her* to the party.

5. *You* need to see *them* as soon as possible.

6. *He* ate dinner with *me*.

Circle the pronoun that correctly completes each sentence. Remember to split the sentence first if it contains a "double" construction. Apply the rules of formal English usage.

7. It was (he, him) who recommended you for the job.

8. The agreement between you and (I, me) requires us to split the rent and the cost of the utilities.

9. (We, us) small business owners worry about providing health insurance for our employees.

10. Her husband and (she, her) enjoy inviting friends over for dinner.

11. Our boss gave Ted and (I, me) a raise last week.

12. The landlord's rent increases made (we, us) tenants angry.

13. If I were (she, her), I'd start looking for a new job.

14. This is a problem that concerns only our neighbors and (we, us).

15. In order for you and (he, him) to attend the concert, you must buy your tickets today.

16. Raising tuition fees would be unfair to (we, us) students.

17. This gift is for (she, her) and her husband.

18. Give the information to Paula and (I, me).

19. The winners of the contest were Bob and (she, her).

20. It is only (they, them) who can help you solve this problem.

Exercise 17B

Some of the following sentences contain pronoun errors. Cross out the incorrect pronouns, and write in the correct forms. If a sentence contains no pronoun errors, label it C for *correct*. Apply the rules of formal English usage.

1. The director told Sarah and I that we were in the play.

2. The summary of the report was published for we employees in the company newsletter.

3. It was her who bought the house down the street from us.

4. The solution to the problem was resolved between Jenny and her co-workers and not between Jenny and I.

5. Ben and her always talk on the phone for hours.

6. Us students need to talk to the college administration about those high student fees.

7. He and me love to play basketball after work.

8. It is them who arrived late for the party, not us.

9. The presentation was written and displayed by Julia, Collin, and I.

10. Bob and her have been dating for several months.

11. Between you and I, the price of our new car was a great deal.

12. The coach assigned Joe and I new positions to play.

13. If I were her, I'd lose a few pounds before I wore that bathing suit.

14. Park the car in the garage and leave the keys with Kevin or they.

15. Barbara and me have been thinking about going to an exercise class.

16. We were surprised when Alan gave Peggy's cousin and I the books on computer design.

17. For all of we students, the change in classroom arrangement seemed a good thing.

18. The movie about the disaster gave us, its viewers, huge nightmares.

19. Although the majority of us wanted to watch horror films, Carrie and us comedy lovers rebelled!

20. Our supervisor wants you and I to finish the report this week.

CHAPTER 18

PRONOUNS IN COMPARISONS AND PRONOUNS WITH *-self, -selves*

USING PRONOUNS IN COMPARISONS

In speech and in writing, we often compare two people or two things with each other. For example,

> *Rose* is older than *I* am.
>
> The company pays *Ellen* a higher salary than it pays *me*.

In the sentences above, it is easy to tell whether a subject pronoun or an object pronoun should be used in each comparison. In the first sentence, the subject pronoun *I* is correct because it would be clearly ungrammatical to say "Rose is older than *me* am." In the second sentence, the object pronoun *me* is correct because you would not say "The company pays Ellen a higher salary than it pays *I*."

When writing, however, people usually do not express comparisons in full, but use a shortened form instead. For example,

> Mary Anne plays tennis better than *I*.
>
> The accident injured Sam more than *me*.

In these cases, it is possible to determine which pronoun is correct by mentally filling in the words that have been left out of the comparison.

Mary Anne plays tennis better than I (do).

The accident injured Sam more than (it injured) me.

Fill in the missing words to determine which pronouns are correct in the following sentences:

Clarence can run longer distances than (I, me).

I enjoy classical music more than (he, him).

This trip will be more interesting for you than (she, her).

That dress looks better on you than (she, her).

Doing sit-ups is easier for you than (I, me).

When you fill in the missing words, the correct comparisons are

Clarence can run longer distances than *I* (can).

I enjoy classical music more than *he* (does).

This trip will be more interesting for you than (it will be for) *her*.

That dress looks better on you than (it does on) *her*.

Doing sit-ups is easier for you than (it is for) *me*.

In *informal* usage, you often hear people use object pronouns instead of subject pronouns in comparisons (for example, "He's taller than me" instead of "He's taller than I"). However, these forms are generally considered inappropriate in writing and formal speech. You should be especially careful in situations where the wrong pronoun can change the meaning of the entire sentence. For example, "Mary danced with George more than *I* (danced with him)" does not mean the same thing as "Mary danced with George more than (she danced with) *me*." In addition, using the wrong pronoun can sometimes lead to unintentionally ridiculous sentences, such as the following:

My husband likes sports more than me.

Unless the husband happens to like sports more than he likes his wife, the correct pronoun would be:

My husband likes sports more than *I* (do).

(Note: The conjunction *than*, which is used in comparisons, should not be confused with the adverb *then*.)

AVOIDING DOUBLED SUBJECTS

Do not "double," or repeat, the subject of a sentence by repeating the noun in its pronoun form.

INCORRECT	My sister, she is a nurse.
CORRECT	My sister is a nurse.
INCORRECT	The Johnsons, they are our neighbors.
CORRECT	The Johnsons are our neighbors.

PRONOUNS WITH -SELF, -SELVES

Some pronouns end in *-self* or *-selves*:

Singular	*Plural*
myself	ourselves
yourself	yourselves
himself	themselves
herself	
itself	

These pronouns can be used in two ways. They can be **reflexive pronouns.** Reflexive pronouns are used when the object of the verb or the object of the preposition is the same person or thing as the subject. For example,

I cut *myself.* (myself = I)

They will do the job by *themselves.* (themselves = they)

Susan enjoyed *herself* at the party. (herself = Susan)

Or they may be used for *emphasis.*

Frank *himself* admits that he is lazy.

Her husband is a famous composer, and she *herself* is a well-known singer.

We *ourselves* are responsible for our decisions.

Notice that the singular forms of reflexive pronouns end in *-self,* and the plural forms end in *-selves.* In standard English, there are no such forms as *hisself,*

17. The lawyer asked my husband and me to meet him at ten o'clock.

18. Susan and us have been friends for more than thirty years.

19. The news came as a shock to they and us.

20. The winners of the contest were Matthew and me.

EXERCISE 18B

Cross out any pronoun errors in the following paragraph, and replace them with the correct pronouns. Apply the rules of formal English usage. This exercise covers the rules in chapters 17 and 18.

Me and my friends decided to visit two very interesting museums in Los Angeles. They're only a couple of blocks from each other, so Kevin, Alan, and myself walked to both. Because Kevin and Alan walk a whole lot faster than me, I had to skip to keep up with themselves. Between you and I, the best museum in Los Angeles is the Petersen Automotive Museum. Us car lovers spend lots of time visiting it. The museum was a gift from Margie and Robert Petersen. As great car lovers, they decided that there ought to be a museum to show how important automobiles have been to us as a culture. They also thought that cars are beautiful, like art objects. No one appreciates the value of cars more than me. When Alan gave Kevin and I tickets, we were thrilled! We always enjoy ourselves at this museum.

I love to walk through the exhibits on the first floor because they trace the history of the first automobile. Kevin enjoys these exhibits more than me. He has a keener sense of history than me and always brings me books to read about historical subjects. Us lovers of history get to walk through the exhibits and dioramas of real-life settings of early Los Angeles. The exhibit loved the most by Alan, Kevin, and I was the one depicting the world's first shopping district. Alan and me laughed at Kevin's joke about how shopping was also an L.A. experience. No one should know more about shopping than him because he loves to buy electronics for hisself. I myself love shopping a whole lot too!

All of we car lovers think that the second floor of the Petersen Museum is also very special. Alan and Kevin like these galleries better than me. There are five rotating galleries with state-of-the-art displays of race cars, classic cars, vintage motorcycles, concept cars, celebrity and movie cars, and auto design and technology. Kevin, Alan, and me have our favorites. Kevin loves the vintage cars, Alan loves the race cars, and I love the movie cars.

After we visit the Petersen Museum, us museum lovers like to walk over to the Page Museum, which is located at the Rancho La Brea Tar Pits. There are actual tar pits where extinct Ice Age plants and animals left their fossils between 10,000 and 40,000 years ago. Alan asked Kevin and myself if scientists still work at the La Brea Tar Pits. Us Page Museum lovers showed Alan the laboratory where actual scientific discoveries still take place. Watching the scientists working was more exciting for Alan than for me. Choosing what is exciting is pretty different for Alan and I. He likes scientific things, but I enjoy more theatrical sights. Us less scientific types really like, for example, the life-size replicas of several extinct mammals. The big mammoths and the saber-toothed tigers scare we viewers just a little. The whole museum experience is something Kevin, Alan, and me value a lot!

CHAPTER 19

AGREEMENT OF PRONOUNS WITH THEIR ANTECEDENTS

AGREEMENT IN NUMBER

Like nouns, pronouns may be either singular or plural, depending on whether they refer to one or more than one person or thing. Following are the subject, object, and possessive pronouns you have learned, divided into singular and plural categories.

Singular Pronouns

Subject	Object	Possessive
I	me	my, mine
you	you	your, yours
he	him	his
she	her	her, hers
it	it	its

211

Plural Pronouns

Subject	*Object*	*Possessive*
we	us	our, ours
you	you	your, yours
they	them	their, theirs

Just as a subject must agree in number with its verb, a pronoun must agree in number with its antecedent. (The **antecedent,** you will remember, is the noun to which the pronoun refers.) In other words, if the antecedent is *singular,* the pronoun must be *singular*. If the antecedent is *plural*, the pronoun must be *plural.*

Study the following sentences, in which both the pronouns and their antecedents have been italicized.

Because the *teacher* is ill, *she* will not be at school today.

Because the *teachers* are ill, *they* will not be at school today.

Obviously, few people would make pronoun agreement errors in the above sentences because *teacher* is clearly singular, and *teachers* is clearly plural. However, people often make pronoun agreement errors in cases like the following:

INCORRECT	If an airline *passenger* wants to be certain not to miss a flight, *they* should arrive at the airport an hour before the scheduled departure time.
CORRECT	If an airline *passenger* wants to be certain not to miss a flight, *he* should arrive at the airport an hour before the scheduled departure time.

Because *passengers* include females as well as males, it would be equally correct to say:

If an airline *passenger* wants to be certain not to miss a flight, *she* should arrive at the airport an hour before the scheduled departure time.

If an airline *passenger* wants to be certain not to miss a flight, *she* or *he* should arrive at the airport an hour before the scheduled departure time.

For a more detailed discussion of the *his* or *her* construction, see the section on "Avoiding Sexist Use of Pronouns" on page 214.

Notice the differences in these sentences:

INCORRECT	Each *student* brought *their* notebook.
CORRECT	Each *student* brought *his* notebook.

What causes people to make mistakes like these? The mistakes may occur because when a writer describes a *passenger,* she is thinking of *passengers* (plural) in general. Similarly, a writer may think of a *student* as *students* in general. Nevertheless, because *passenger* and *student* are singular nouns, they must be used with singular pronouns.

Notice that if several pronouns refer to the same antecedent, all of the pronouns must agree in number with that antecedent.

Before Mike begins to run, *he* always stretches *his* muscles.

If the *students* don't review *their* lessons, *they* won't do well on *their* final exams.

Another common pronoun agreement error involves **indefinite pronouns.** As you learned in Chapter 6 on subject-verb agreement, indefinite pronouns are *singular* and require *singular* verbs. (For example, "Everyone *is* happy," *not* "Everyone *are* happy.") Similarly, when indefinite pronouns are used as antecedents, they require *singular* subject, object, and possessive pronouns.

The following words are singular indefinite pronouns:

sing.

anybody, anyone, anything

each, each one

either, neither

everybody, everyone, everything

nobody, no one, nothing

somebody, someone, something

Notice the use of singular pronouns with these words:

Everyone did as *he* pleased.

Somebody has forgotten *her* purse.

Either of the choices has *its* disadvantages.

In informal spoken English, plural pronouns are often used with indefinite pronoun antecedents. However, this construction is generally not considered appropriate in formal speech or writing.

| INFORMAL | *Somebody* should let you borrow *their* book. |
| FORMAL | *Somebody* should let you borrow *his* book. |

In some sentences, an indefinite pronoun is so clearly plural in meaning that a singular pronoun sounds awkward with it. For example,

Everyone on this block must be wealthy because he or she drives a Lexus or a Mercedes-Benz.

A better wording for this sentence would be:

The people on this block must be wealthy because they all drive a Lexus or a Mercedes-Benz.

AVOIDING SEXIST USE OF PRONOUNS

Although matching singular pronouns with singular antecedents is a grammatical problem, a usage problem may occur if the antecedent of a singular pronoun refers to both genders. In the past, singular masculine pronouns were used to refer to antecedents such as *worker* or *student* even if these antecedents included women as well as men. Now, writers prefer to use forms that include both sexes, such as *he* or *she* or *his* or *her* to avoid excluding women.

Notice the difference between the first sentence below and its revisions.

A good doctor always treats *his* patients with respect.

This sentence suggests that all doctors are men. The sentence may be revised by substituting a plural noun and pronoun.

Good doctors always treat *their* patients with respect.

It is also possible to rewrite the sentence so that it no longer contains a pronoun.

Good doctors always treat patients with respect.

How could you reword the following sentence so that it includes both men and women?

Every soldier who is injured in combat is entitled to free medical care for his injuries.

AGREEMENT IN PERSON

In grammar, pronouns are classified into groups called **persons. First person** refers to the person who is speaking. **Second person** refers to the person being spoken to. **Third person** refers to the person or thing being spoken about. Below is a chart of subject pronouns grouped according to person.

	Singular	*Plural*
First person	I	we
Second person	you	you
Third person	he, she, it	they

All nouns are considered third person (either singular or plural) because nouns can be replaced by third-person pronouns (for example, *Susie* = *she*; *a car* = *it*; *babysitters* = *they*).

Just as a pronoun and its antecedent must agree in number, they must also agree in person. Agreement in person becomes a problem only when the second-person pronoun *you* is incorrectly used with a third-person antecedent. Study the following examples:

INCORRECT	If *anyone* wants to vote, *you* must register first.
CORRECT	If *anyone* wants to vote, *he* or *she* must register first.
INCORRECT	When *drivers* get caught in a traffic jam, *you* become impatient.
CORRECT	When *drivers* get caught in a traffic jam, *they* become impatient.

This type of mistake is called a **shift in person** and is considered a serious grammatical error.

In addition to avoiding shifts in person within individual sentences, you should try to be consistent in your use of person when you are writing essays. In general, an entire essay is written in the same person. If, for example, you are writing an essay about the special problems faced by students who work full time, you will probably use either the first or the third person. You should avoid shifts into the second person (*you*) because *you* refers to the reader of your paper and not to the students you are writing about.

INCORRECT	*Students* who work full time have special concerns. For example, *you* must arrange *your* classes to fit *your* work schedule.
CORRECT	*Students* who work full time have special concerns. For example, *they* must arrange *their* classes to fit *their* work schedule.

Circle the pronoun that correctly completes each sentence.

The zoo has extended its hours so that patrons may visit when (your, his, their) schedules allow.

Participants must bring tickets to the front office, or else (you, he, they) will forfeit (your, his, their) chance to win the free gift.

Pay close attention; (your, his, their) final exam grade depends on following the directions carefully.

19B rules

EXERCISE 19A

Part One: Circle the pronoun that best completes each sentence. Apply the rules of formal English usage. These sentences cover only the rules in Chapter 19.

1. Somebody left (his, their) keys in the library.

2. Neither of the companies offers (its, their) customers free shipping.

3. If dieters want to lose weight, (you, (they)) should exercise as well as count calories.

4. No one knows (his, their) final grade yet.

5. Each of the mothers enrolled (her, their) children in a preschool.

6. An attorney can look forward to earning a good salary during (his, his or her, their) career.

7. Everybody on the committee needs to turn in (your, her, their) report by Friday.

8. Some students may have to drop out of school if the college raises (your, their) tuition.

9. Has anybody forgotten to sign (your, (his,) their) time card?

10. If a driver has too many tickets, (she, they) will have to pay more for (her, their) insurance.

Part Two: This section covers rules from Chapters 17 through 19. If a sentence contains a pronoun error, cross out the incorrect pronoun and write in the correct form. Some sentences may contain more than one error. If a sentence contains no pronoun errors, label it *C* for *correct*. Apply the rules of formal English usage and try to avoid sexist use of pronouns.

11. If a veteran has a combat-related injury, his medical care should be paid for by the government.

12. You play the piano better than me.

13. Please leave the package with either our neighbors or us.

14. You need to tell my husband and I where to meet you.

15. Us parents are concerned about our children's school.

16. The boss gave she and her assistant a bonus for completing the project a month early.

17. The school will ask Judy and myself to provide refreshments at the next meeting.

18. The students did all of the work by themselfs.

19. Our neighbors and us are going to Hawaii next month.

20. You promised to do all the work, but it is us who ended up finishing the job.

21. The police officer asked the other driver and I to pull over to the side of the road.

22. The reward for finding the lost dog will be divided between you and I.

Exercise 19B

If a sentence contains a pronoun error, cross out the incorrect error, and write in the correct pronoun. If a sentence contains no errors, label it *C* for *correct*. Some sentences should be reworded so that they do not refer exclusively to men. Apply the rules of formal English usage. This exercise covers rules from Chapters 17 through 19.

1. Each applicant must send their resume to the manager of the company.

2. My roommate studied a lot more than I for the chemistry exam.

3. Either Julia or Liz will send their report to the manager.

4. We wanted to help them paint their house, but they decided to do it themselfs.

5. When students arrive late to class, you find it difficult to follow the lecture.

6. Our friends don't own as many computers as us.

7. Each applicant for the new position placed his information in the file on the left.

8. The majority of the students need work full-time.

9. Anybody can forget their homework at least once a semester!

10. Us sports fans always get together to watch the Super Bowl.

11. When my boss gave my co-worker and I a raise, she was more grateful than I.

12. Before students prepare for a big exam, you should find a quiet place to study.

13. The election was a tie between Sarah and I.

14. Somebody left their purse near the bus station.

15. Distribute the homework to they and the other class.

16. The newscaster chose John and myself to interview for the article.

17. Each pregnant woman received their pre-natal care at the county hospital.

18. Please give the rent payment to my husband or myself by the end of this week.

19. If citizens want to make their voices heard, you should always vote.

20. Each professor provided his students with a detailed course schedule.

C H A P T E R 20

ORDER OF PRONOUNS
AND SPELLING OF POSSESSIVES

ORDER OF PRONOUNS

When you are referring to someone else and to yourself in the same sentence, mention the other person's name (or the pronoun that replaces the name) before you mention your own.

INCORRECT	*I* and *George* are brothers.
CORRECT	*George* and *I* are brothers.
INCORRECT	You can borrow five dollars from *me* or *her*.
CORRECT	You can borrow five dollars from *her* or *me*.

The construction is actually not a rule of grammar; rather, it is considered a matter of courtesy.

Possessive Pronouns

Here is a list of possessive pronouns that you have already studied. This time, look carefully at how they are spelled and punctuated.

221

	Singular	*Plural*
First person	my, mine	our, ours
Second person	your, yours	your, yours
Third person	his	their, theirs
	her, hers	
	its	

Possessive pronouns do not contain apostrophes.

INCORRECT	The beach blanket was her's.
CORRECT	The beach blanket was hers.

Be especially careful not to confuse the possessive pronoun *its* with the contraction *it's* (it is).

INCORRECT	The car wouldn't start because *it's* battery was dead.
CORRECT	The car wouldn't start because *its* battery was dead.

Another source of confusion is the apostrophe, which indicates the omitted letters in contractions. For example, the apostrophe in *don't* represents the missing *o* from *do not*. Some contractions of pronouns and verbs have the same pronunciations as certain possessive pronouns. These pairs of words sound alike but differ in meaning. Don't confuse them in your writing.

who's–whose

Who's he? = *Who is* he?
Whose magazine is this? (possessive)

you're–your

You're looking well. = *You are* looking well.
Your car has a flat tire. (possessive)

they're–their

They're coming to the party. = *They are* coming to the party.
Their exhibit won the prize. (possessive)

Circle the pronoun that correctly completes each sentence.

That dog is (hers, her's).

(Whose, Who's) car is blocking the driveway?

The team just received (its, it's) award.

(Your, You're) a happy person.

The new house is (theirs, their's).

A final note: When you do pronoun exercises, or when you use pronouns in your own writing, remember to apply the rules you have learned. If you rely on what "sounds right," your instincts may supply only those pronouns that would be appropriate in *informal* English.

EXERCISE 20A

their = poss

If a sentence contains a pronoun error, cross out the incorrect pronoun, and write in the correct form. Some sentences may contain more than one error. If a sentence contains no pronoun errors, label it *C* for *correct*. Apply the rules of formal English usage. Sentences 1–10 cover only the rules from Chapter 20.

1. ~~Whose~~ *Who's* helping you paint your house?

2. I was sure that the mistake was hers. *C*

3. Jon and Kate aren't here yet; ~~their~~ *they're* caught in a traffic jam.

4. The hurricane left flooded streets and destroyed houses in ~~its~~ *its* wake.

5. I don't know ~~who's~~ *whose* car is parked by the fire hydrant.

6. Please notify ~~you're~~ *your* supervisor if your going to be late.

7. The large house at the end of the block is ~~ours~~ *ours*.

8. ~~I and my husband~~ *my husband & I* would like to invite you to dinner.

9. ~~Your's~~ *Yours* is the winning entry in the contest.

10. ~~Its~~ *It's* not easy to attend college and work full-time too.

The following sentences cover rules from Chapters 17 through 20.

11. ~~Its~~ *It's* getting more difficult to find qualified math and science teachers.

12. Matt has lived in this neighborhood a lot longer than ~~me~~ *I*.

13. My older sister and ~~myself~~ *me* are planning a surprise party for our parents.

14. When a woman loses their job, ~~they~~ *she* may also lose their health insurance.

15. The children asked their father and I if they could go to a movie this afternoon. *C*

16. It is ~~us~~ *we*, not our neighbors, who need a ride to the game tomorrow.

17. ~~As~~ *We* senior citizens need to make sure that we stay physically active as we age.

18. I think that the economic downturn has affected ~~our~~ *his* parents more than us.

19. We were both injured in the car accident, but my husband was more badly hurt than ~~me~~ *I*.

20. If anyone plans to visit Canada or Mexico, ~~they~~ *he* must have a passport.

EXERCISE 20B

[handwritten: for thursday]

If a sentence contains a pronoun error, cross out the incorrect pronoun, and write in the correct form. Some sentences may contain more than one error. If a sentence contains no errors, label it *C* for *correct*. Apply the rules of formal English usage. This exercise covers rules from Chapters 17 through 20.

1. ~~Whose~~ *[Who's]* making all the noise in the basement?

2. Everyone should exercise ~~their~~ *[his]* right to vote.

3. I and my classmates want to create a website for our project.

4. If I were as talented as her, I'd write the great American novel! *C*

5. ~~Its~~ *[It's]* not safe to leave your door unlocked when you go away.

6. Your the best athlete on this team, so please don't transfer to another school. *C*

7. That cute little puppy with the pink ribbon must be ~~their's~~ *[theirs]*.

8. The homeless men don't know where ~~their~~ *[they're]* going to sleep tonight.

9. The rock star gave Billy and I his autograph. *C*

10. ~~Anyone~~ who works hard should have ~~their~~ *[his]* efforts rewarded.

11. Although I practice guitar every day, Johnny plays a whole lot better than ~~me~~ *[I]*.

12. Did you give that beautiful bouquet of flowers to Maggie and me? *C*

13. No one knew ~~who's~~ *[whose]* keys were left on the dining room table.

14. My ~~mother's~~ *[mothers]* cat loves to scratch ~~its~~ *[it's]* paws on her brand new couch.

15. Making Thanksgiving dinner is a lot of fun, but sometimes its just so much easier to have someone who cooks better than us take over. *C*

16. ~~Myself and John~~ *[John and me]* drove across the country in his old VW van.

17. ~~There's~~ *there's* no reason why people shouldn't speak up for what you believe.

18. ~~Its~~ *it's* my fault that the dinner burned and the party was a failure!

19. That backpack doesn't look like mine, so it must be ~~your's.~~ *yours*

20. ~~Its~~ *it's* important to know whether students failed the exam because of its difficulty or because of its length.

UNIT 5 REVIEW

Part One: Correct any pronoun errors in the following paragraphs. Cross out the incorrect pronouns, and write in the correct forms. Apply the rules of formal English usage.

Life is difficult now for my children and myself because I am temporarily a single mother. My husband, he is in Iraq on his second tour of duty there, so my children and I have to take care of ourselfs here at home.

I miss my husband a lot, but the children miss him even more than me. It is especially hard for my thirteen-year-old son. His father and him often did things together, like going to baseball games and working in the yard. Last weekend our church had a father–son bowling night. My son went with my older brother. Later on, my son said, "I'm glad that Uncle Frank could go bowling with me, but Dad is a much better bowler than him."

My sixteen-year-old daughter misses her father too. Every teenage girl needs to have their father around. My daughter and her boyfriend had an argument today. If her father were home, it would be him talking to her about the way teenaged boys act instead of her getting advice from only her younger brother and I.

When a person is a single mother, every problem and every responsibility ends up in your lap. Us military wives are accustomed to being left alone while our husbands are on active duty, but our children are less resilient than us. Its the children who's fathers are gone who suffer the most.

CHAPTER 21

CAPITALIZATION

The general principle behind capitalization is that **proper nouns** (names of *specific* persons, places, or things) are capitalized. **Common nouns** (names of *general* persons, places, or things) are *not* capitalized.

Study the following sentences, each of which illustrates a rule of capitalization.

1. Capitalize all parts of a person's name.

   That man is *John Allen Ford*.

2. Capitalize the titles of relatives only when the titles precede the person's name or when they take the place of a person's name.

   Our favorite relative is *Uncle Max*.
   Are you ready, *Mother*?
   but
   My *m*other and *f*ather are retired.

The same rule applies to professional titles.

> We saw *Doctor Johnson* at the market.
> but
> I must see a *doctor* soon.

3. Capitalize the names of streets, cities, and states.

> Deirdre moved to 418 *Palm Avenue*, *Placerville*, *California*.

4. Capitalize the names of countries, languages, and ethnic groups.

> The two languages spoken most frequently in *Switzerland* are *German* and *French*, but some *Swiss* also speak *Italian*.

5. Capitalize the names of specific buildings, geographical features, schools, and other institutions.

> They visited the *Tower of London*, the *Thames River*, and *Cambridge University*.

6. Capitalize the days of the week, the months of the year, and the names of holidays. Do not capitalize the names of the seasons of the year.

> *Monday, February 14*, is *Valentine's Day*.
> My favorite time of the year is the *fall*, especially *November*.

7. Capitalize directions of the compass only when they refer to specific regions.

> Her accent revealed that she had been brought up in the *South*.
> Philadelphia is *south* of New York City.

8. Capitalize the names of companies and brand names but not the names of the products themselves.

> *General Foods Corporation* manufactures *Yuban* coffee.
> We love *Campbell's* soups.

9. Capitalize the first word of every sentence.
10. Capitalize the subject pronoun I.

11. Capitalize the first word of a title and all other words in the title except for articles (a, an, the) and except for conjunctions and prepositions that have fewer than five letters.

    I loved the novel *The House of the Seven Gables* by Nathaniel Hawthorne.

    I enjoy reading the short essay "*Once More to the Lake.*"

12. Capitalize the names of academic subjects only if they are already proper nouns or if they are common nouns followed by a course number.

    Her schedule of classes includes *c*alculus, *E*nglish, and *P*sychology 101.

13. Capitalize the names of specific historical events, such as wars, revolutions, religious and political movements, and specific eras.

    The *R*oaring *T*wenties came to an end with the start of the *D*epression.

    Martin Luther was a key figure in the *P*rotestant *R*eformation.

    My grandfather was wounded in the *B*attle of the *B*ulge during *W*orld *W*ar *T*wo.

      f. to show separate ownership, add an apostrophe plus *s* to both nouns

            George Washington's and Thomas Jefferson's signatures

3. before a gerund (an *–ing* form of a verb being used as a noun)

     My sister's smoking led to her death from lung cancer.

     Tim's being at the party was a surprise to the other guests.

4. to show the omission of numbers in a date

     the Roaring '20s   the class of '98

5. to form the plurals of letters and of academic titles

     p's and q's   M.A.'s

Writers sometimes use an apostrophe where it is *not* needed. Be careful not to make the following kinds of errors.

1. Do not use apostrophes with possessive pronouns.

     error: That book is *her's*.

     correct: That book is *hers*.

     error: The dog wagged *it's* tail.

     correct: The dog wagged *its* tail.

2. Do not use an apostrophe to form a plural noun that is *not* possessive.

     error: Professional *athletes'* earn a lot of money.

     correct: Professional *athletes* earn a lot of money.

     error: Happy holidays from the *Chandler's*

     correct: Happy holidays from the *Chandlers*

DIRECT QUOTATIONS

Direct quotations make writing vivid. Most direct quotations are simply enclosed in **quotation marks.**

    "Give me liberty, or give me death."

If the quotation is part of a longer sentence, it is set off by commas.

> Patrick Henry said, "Give me liberty, or give me death."
> "Friends," the speaker said, "it's time for a new beginning."

Three rules govern the use of quotation marks with other forms of punctuation:

1. The comma and period are always placed *inside* the quotation marks.

   The class read "Fern Hill," a poem by Dylan Thomas.

2. The colon and semicolon are always placed *outside* the quotation marks.

   I love the song "Blue"; it was recorded by LeAnn Rimes.

3. Question marks, exclamation marks, and dashes are placed *inside* the quotation marks if they apply only to the quoted material and *after* the quotation marks if they apply to the whole sentence.

   "Is dinner almost ready?" asked Beth.

   Did Shakespeare say, "The ripeness is all"?

QUOTATION MARKS VERSUS ITALICS

[handwritten annotations: — Book, newspaper etc. • sovereign words • word-as-word • publication comes out as a separate publication]

You may have noticed in the discussion of capitalization that some titles are punctuated with quotation marks ("Once More to the Lake"), and some titles are shown in *italics (The House of the Seven Gables)*. The choice between these two ways to indicate titles is generally based on the length of the work. The titles of short works, such as songs, short poems and stories, essays and articles in periodicals, and episodes of a series, are put between *quotation marks*. The titles of longer works, such as full-length books and the names of newspapers, magazines, movies, television shows, and the titles of complete volumes or complete series, are put in *italics*.

Italics are a special slanted typeface used by printers. In a handwritten or typewritten paper, italics must be indicated by **underlining.**

> We read the chapter "No Name Woman" from Maxine Hong Kingston's *The Woman Warrior.*

> She sang the song "Summertime" from *Porgy and Bess.*

> Did you see the episode "The Coming of Shadows" on the television series *Babylon 5?*

> *The Los Angeles Times* printed an article titled "Upsetting Our Sense of Self" on the way cloning may influence how we think about our identity.

Exercise 22B

Part One: Add the following punctuation marks to the sentences wherever they are needed: commas, colons, dashes, quotation marks, apostrophes, and italics. Use dashes to punctuate abrupt parenthetical expressions. Indicate italics by *underlining*.

1. I love listening to older rock songs the Beatles and Metallica especially.

2. I have three favorite Metallica songs One, And Justice for All, and To Live Is to Die.

3. My sister-in-laws favorite activity is to play her guitar and sing old rock songs.

4. All of my friends loved reading the Twilight novels and can't wait for the next film version.

5. Seeing that the ticket line was too long, we decided to see the movie The Informant another night.

6. Charlotte's Web is my favorite childrens book, and its also a great American classic.

7. The storys ending still makes me cry although I have read the book many times.

8. It also has one of the most famous first lines in children's literature when Fern asks Wheres Papa going with that ax?

9. In the novel The Lion, the Witch, and the Wardrobe, my favorite chapter is titled Deeper Magic From Beyond the Dawn of Time.

10. My sisters both have M.A.s in biology, and they are both members of the class of 99.

11. Sarahs and Jennifers first jobs were in emergency rooms in very busy urban hospitals.

12. Have you ever read the short story A Late Encounter with the Enemy by Flannery O'Connor?

13. In addition to liking the short stories by O'Connor, I also enjoy reading stories by the following writers Ernest Hemingway, James Joyce, and Joyce Carol Oates.

14. An article in the New York Times op-ed section titled Pun for the Ages by Joseph Tartakovsky argued for and against using puns.

15. The article quotes the following famous pun They say that the pun is the lowest form of wit. But theres verse!

16. My mother and fathers favorite restaurant just closed.

17. That habit of hers chewing gum very loudly is bound to bring her the wrong kind of attention.

18. One of my all-time favorite television shows was I Love Lucy, especially the episode entitled Lucy Does a TV Commercial.

19. We all have our favorite television shows, dont we?

Part Two: The following paragraph contains both capitalization errors and errors involving the use of some of the following punctuation marks: commas, colons, dashes, quotation marks, italics, and apostrophes. Correct any errors you find. Indicate italics by *underlining*.

Because I love detective fiction stories, I wanted to learn all about raymond chandler, one of the greatest of all pulp fiction writers. He created the down and out detective philip marlowe, a tough guy with a soft side. Marlowe has the following traits hes a tough guy but sometimes sentimental, has few friend's, went to a university, speaks a little spanish, and likes chess and classical music. I love his language because its the perfect hardboiled style we associate with this kind of story. one of my favorite lines is The muzzle of the Luger looked like the mouth of the Second street tunnel. That description is just perfect Chandler prose. Even his biography sounds a little like a novel that he could have written. He was born in the united states, but wound up living in great Britain. His father an alcoholic abandoned him, but his wealthy uncle supported the family. He attended dulwich college, london, traveled to paris and munich, worked as a civil servant, became a newspaper reporter for the daily express newspaper, and returned to the united states to find his fortune. After world war I he returned to los angeles and began to earn a living by writing. His first short story, blackmailers don't shoot, was published in black mask magazine in 1933. His first novel, the big sleep, was published in 1939. It was a huge success and became a film with humphrey bogart playing philip marlowe. Chandler has became famous for pulp fiction stories about los angeles in the 30s and 40s. In addition to writing novels, short fiction, and films, chandler also wrote magazine articles for the atlantic monthly. One of the most famous of these articles is the simple art of murder, published in 1945. Even his death was like a story. Because of a lawsuit concerning his estate, chandler was never buried next to his beloved wife cissy something he had wanted.

CHAPTER 23

Misplaced and Dangling Modifiers

Modifiers are words that are used to describe other words in a sentence. A modifier may be a single word, a phrase, or a clause. (Adjective clauses are discussed in Chapter 15.) Examples of some of the more common types of modifiers are given below. Circle the word that each italicized modifier describes.

ADJECTIVE	He drank a cup of *black* coffee.
ADJECTIVE CLAUSE	The woman *who is dressed in blue* is the bride's mother.
PREPOSITIONAL PHRASE	*With the help of a nurse,* the patient was able to take a shower.

The words you should have circled are *coffee*, which is modified by "black," *woman*, which is modified by "who is dressed in blue," and *patient*, which is modified by "with the help of a nurse."

Another type of modifier is a **participial phrase.** A participial phrase begins with a participle. A **participle** is a verb form that functions as an adjective. There are two kinds of participles. **Present participles** are formed by adding *-ing* to the main verb (for example, *walking, knowing, seeing*). **Past participles** are the verb forms that are used with the helping verb *have* (have *walked*, have *known*, have *seen*). Circle the word that each of the following participial phrases modifies.

Looking excited, the child begged for more presents.

The woman *dressed very expensively* is a famous model.

The words that you should have circled are *child* and *woman.*

If you look back at all the words that you have circled so far in this chapter, you will notice that although modifiers sometimes precede and sometimes follow the words they describe, they are in all cases placed as closely as possible to the word that they describe. Failure to place a modifier in the correct position in a sentence results in an error known as a **misplaced modifier.**

MISPLACED	He told a joke to his friends *that no one liked.* (Did no one like his friends?)
CORRECT	He told a joke *that no one liked* to his friends.
MISPLACED	Sue always uses pencils for her math exams *with extremely fine points.* (Do the exams have extremely fine points?)
CORRECT	Sue always uses pencils *with extremely fine points* for her math exams.

Correct the misplaced modifiers in the following sentences.

The citizen informed the sheriff that the thief had escaped by phone.

The child clutched the old teddy bear with tears rolling down his face.

A firm called Threshold provides companions for people who are dying at $7.50 per hour.

An error related to the misplaced modifier is the **dangling modifier.** A dangling modifier sometimes occurs when a participial phrase is placed at the beginning of a sentence. A participial phrase in this position *must describe the subject of the following clause.* If the subject of the clause cannot logically perform the action described in the participial phrase, the phrase is said to "dangle" (to hang loosely, without a logical connection).

EXERCISE 23B

Part One: Some of the following sentences contain misplaced modifiers or dangling modifiers. Rewrite these sentences. If a sentence is already correctly constructed, label it C for *correct*.

1. Studying for my final exams, my eyes grew tired and blurry.

   _____

   _____

2. Sara bought a birthday gift at the corner store wrapped in brightly colored paper.

   _____

   _____

3. Waiting at the stop light, my car's battery stopped working!

   _____

   _____

4. The sale at the department store advertised great bargains at the corner of Fifth Street and Vine.

   _____

   _____

5. Wanting to be petted some more, the puppy cuddled close to us.

   _____

   _____

6. John gave his girlfriend a wedding ring with beautiful long, brown hair.

   _____

   _____

7. After washing the dinner dishes, some good moisturizing lotion will help your hands feel better.

_____

_____

8. I completed the assignment for this week's psychology class at the neighborhood coffee shop.

_____

_____

9. After winning the race, the party at the club went on for hours.

_____

_____

10. The teacher persuaded the student to study harder for the test that was having a difficult time.

_____

_____

Part Two: Correct any misplaced or dangling modifiers in the following paragraph.

While driving to school, my car broke down. The mechanic told me that the car needed a lot of new parts at the neighborhood garage. After diagnosing the problem, the battery and the alternator both needed to be replaced. I calculated the cost of this repair and was astonished at the expense. I decided that I should try to get a second estimate. However, having mechanical problems, I couldn't really get my car to another shop. I then considered buying a bicycle to ride to school to save myself money. Being out of shape, the ten-mile trip to campus didn't seem like a good idea. After thinking a while, my next idea to save money was to use public transportation. However I would have to walk at least two miles to the nearest bus stop in the snow. Knowing my physical laziness, walking any distance in the snow wouldn't work out! Just as I was falling into despair, the mechanic called me with news that made me happy. After searching around, a refurbished battery and alternator appeared. The cost was just right for my pocketbook for the repairs!

C H A P T E R 24

PARALLEL STRUCTURE

he term **parallel structure** means that similar ideas should be expressed in similar grammatical structures. For example, Benjamin Franklin quoted the following proverb:

Early to bed and early to rise make a man healthy, wealthy, and wise.

This proverb is a good illustration of parallel structure. It begins with two similar phrases, "Early to bed" and "early to rise," and it ends with a series of three similar words (they are all adjectives): *healthy, wealthy,* and *wise.*

In contrast, the following two versions of the same proverb contain some words that are *not* parallel.

Early to bed and early *rising* make a man healthy, wealthy, and wise.

Early to bed and early to rise make a man healthy, wealthy, and *give him wisdom.*

Therefore, these last two sentences are not properly constructed.

Because there are many different grammatical structures in the English language, the possibilities for constructing nonparallel sentences may appear to be almost unlimited. Fortunately, you do not have to be able to identify all the grammatical structures in a sentence to tell whether or not that sentence has parallel structure. Sentences that lack parallel structure are usually so awkward that they are easy to recognize.

NOT PARALLEL	My chores *are washing dishes, cleaning the bathrooms, and to water the lawn.*
PARALLEL	My chores are *washing dishes, cleaning the bathrooms, and watering the lawn.*
NOT PARALLEL	I expect you *to read* all the assignments, *to complete all the exercises*, and *that you should attend every class.*
PARALLEL	I expect you *to read* all the assignments, *to complete* all the exercises, and *to attend* every class.
NOT PARALLEL	The fortune teller said my husband would be *tall, dark, and have good looks.*
PARALLEL	The fortune teller said my husband would be *tall, dark,* and *good-looking.*

Revise each of the following sentences so that it is parallel in structure.

The steak was tough, overcooked, and had no taste.

The school emphasizes the basic skills of reading, how to write, and arithmetic.

He spent his day off playing tennis and went to the beach.

Your blind date is attractive and has intelligence.

Some errors in parallel structure occur when a writer is not careful in the use of correlative conjunctions. **Correlative conjunctions** are conjunctions that occur in pairs, such as:

both . . . and

either . . . or

neither . . . nor

not only . . . but also

Because these conjunctions occur in pairs, they are usually used to compare two ideas. For example,

> My professor suggests that I *not only* study more *but also* attend class more regularly.

Correctly used, correlative conjunctions will structure a sentence in effective parallel form.

The rule for using correlative conjunctions is that the conjunctions *must be placed as closely as possible to the words that are being compared*. For example,

> I must go home *either* today *or* tomorrow.
>
>   not
>
> I *either* must go home today *or* tomorrow.

Study the following examples of correctly and incorrectly placed correlative conjunctions.

INCORRECT	He *not only* got an "A" in math *but also* in English.
CORRECT	He got an "A" *not only* in math *but also* in English.
INCORRECT	She *neither* is a good housekeeper *nor* a good cook.
CORRECT	She is *neither* a good housekeeper *nor* a good cook.

Correct the misplaced correlative conjunctions in the following sentences.

He both collects stamps and coins.

She neither eats meat nor dairy products.

He both plays the piano and the flute.

My daughter not only has had chicken pox but also mumps.

Exercise 24A

Part One: Rewrite any sentences that lack parallel structure. If a sentence is already parallel, label it *C* for *correct*.

1. The police officer asked me to pull over to the curb and that I should show him my driver's license.

   _____

   _____

2. Did Patrick Henry ask either to be given liberty or death?

   _____

   _____

3. She uses her free time for exercising and to do volunteer work.

   _____

   _____

4. This house not only has a swimming pool but also a hot tub.

   _____

   _____

5. The hotel employees were told that they should speak politely to the guests and to smile.

   _____

   _____

6. The cafeteria serves food that is tasty, nutritious, and doesn't cost very much.

   _____

   _____

7. This unit has covered parallel structure, punctuation, and how to capitalize.

_____

_____

8. The politician's speech was long, boring, and uninformative.

_____

_____

9. The company wanted to hire someone who was competent, experienced, and who had enthusiasm.

_____

_____

10. I like to study subjects that relate to my life, that give me insight into myself, and are helping me to understand my world better.

_____

_____

Part Two: Use the directions for each item to write sentences of your own that have correct parallel structure.

11. Use a series of three adjectives to describe someone you know. (*My friend is*

_____, _____, and _____.)

_____

_____

12. Use a series of three infinitives (verb forms beginning with *to*, like *to write*) to describe three things that you need to do this weekend.

_____

_____

13. Write a sentence that contains the correctly placed correlative conjunctions *either . . . or.*

    _____

    _____

14. Use a series of three gerunds (-ing verb forms, like *swimming*) to describe things that you enjoy doing during your free time.

    _____

    _____

15. Write a sentence that contains the correctly placed correlative conjunctions *not only . . . but also.*

    _____

    _____

CHAPTER 25

IRREGULAR VERBS

erbs have three **principal** (meaning "most important") **parts**: the *present* (which, when preceded by *to,* becomes the *infinitive*), the *past,* and the *past participle.*

The **present** form may stand alone as a main verb without any helping verb. For example,

I *like* movies.

We *watch* television each night.

It may also be preceded by a helping verb, such as *can, could, do, does, did, may, might, must, shall, should, will,* or *would.* (A list of helping verbs appears in Chapter 4.)

I *must talk* with you tomorrow.

Julia *should study* her vocabulary words.

However, the present form is not used after any forms of the helping verbs *have* (*has, have, had*) or *be* (*am, is, are, was, were, been*). The **past participle** (see below) is used after these verbs.

The **past** form is used alone as a main verb. It is *not* preceded by a helping verb when expressing the simple past tense.

They *ran* back to the classroom.

We *spelled* all the words correctly.

The **past participle** is preceded by at least one, and sometimes more than one, helping verb. The helping verb is often a form of *have* or *be*.

She *has spoken* very kindly of you.

The batter *was hit* by a ball.

Joe *had* always *been* poor until he won the lottery.

Most English verbs are **regular.** A regular verb forms both its past and past participle by adding *-ed* to the present. (If the present already ends in *-e*, only a *-d* is added.)

Present	*Past*	*Past Participle*
walk	walked	walked
live	lived	lived

Any verb that does *not* form both its past and past participle by adding *-ed* or *-d* is considered **irregular.** For example,

Present	*Past*	*Past Participle*
fall	fell	fallen
give	gave	given
hide	hid	hidden

Because irregular verbs by definition have irregular spellings, you must *memorize* the spelling of their past and past participle forms. Irregular verbs include many of the most commonly used verbs in the English language (for example, *come, go, eat, drink, sit, stand*), so it is important to study them carefully.

Several pairs of verbs are often confused: *lie/lay, sit/set,* and *rise/raise.*

The irregular verb *lie* means to recline or to be in a horizontal position.

I *lie* down whenever I feel dizzy.

The verb *lay* means to put something down. This verb always has a direct object.

> *Lay* your cards on the table.
>
> The hen *laid* six eggs.

(Notice that the verb *lie,* meaning to say something that is not true, is a *regular* verb: *lie, lied, lied.*)

The verb *sit* means to be in a seated position.

> I always *sit* in the front row of a classroom.

One meaning of the verb *set* is to put something in a particular place. When it is used in this sense, *set* has a direct object.

> She always *sets* her table with fine china and linen napkins.
>
> He *set* the clocks an hour ahead last night.
>
> The verb *rise* means to get up or go higher.

> The audience *rose* to sing the national anthem.
>
> The sun *rises* at seven A.M.

One meaning of the verb *raise* is to lift something higher or to increase it. When used in this sense, *raise* has a direct object.

> After we *raise* the curtain, the performance will begin.
>
> The store *raised* its prices after the sale ended.

The verb *raise* is regular: *raise, raised, raised.*

Here is a list of some of the most commonly used irregular verbs. In addition to learning the verbs on this list, if you are not sure whether or not a verb is irregular, look it up in the dictionary. A good dictionary will list the principal parts of an irregular verb in addition to defining its meaning.

Present	*Past*	*Past Participle*
beat	beat	beaten
begin	began	begun
bend	bent	bent
bleed	bled	bled

Present	*Past*	*Past Participle*
blow	blew	blown
break	broke	broken
bring	brought	brought
build	built	built
buy	bought	bought
catch	caught	caught
choose	chose	chosen
come	came	come
cut	cut	cut
do	did	done
draw	drew	drawn
drink	drank	drunk
drive	drove	driven
eat	ate	eaten
fall	fell	fallen
feed	fed	fed
feel	felt	felt
find	found	found
fly	flew	flown
freeze	froze	frozen
get	got	got *or* gotten
give	gave	given
go	went	gone
grow	grew	grown
have	had	had
hear	heard	heard
hide	hid	hidden
hit	hit	hit
hurt	hurt	hurt
keep	kept	kept
know	knew	known
lay	laid	laid

22. She was (hit) _____ by a car while she was crossing a street in a clearly marked crosswalk.

23. The driver (leave) _____ the scene without stopping, and Anna (lie) _____ on the street for several minutes before she was (see) _____ by a passerby.

24. She was (take) _____ to a hospital where doctors (find) _____ that she (have) _____ a concussion and a (break) _____ leg.

25. She (spend) _____ three days in the hospital before her doctor (give) her _____ permission to go home.

26. The missing driver has not been (find) _____, and the police have (tell) _____ Anna that they do not think he will ever be arrested.

27. Anna (weep) _____ when I (speak) _____ to her on the phone last week.

28. She has not (sleep) _____ well since her accident, and her broken leg has (keep) _____ her at home, away from her job.

29. However, her friends have (take) _____ good care of Anna.

30. They have (come) _____ to visit her every day and have (bring) _____ food for her to eat.

31. They have also (do) _____ her housework and have (lend) _____ her books and magazines to read.

32. Their help has (mean) _____ a lot to Anna, who has recently (begin) _____ to feel better.

Exercise 25B

Grammar Note: The **past perfect tense** is formed by using the helping verb *had* plus the past participle of the main verb. The past perfect is used if you are already writing in the past tense and need to refer to an action that happened even earlier.

Collin took just a short nap this afternoon because he *had taken* a long nap this morning.

Barbara *had* already *studied* for several hours when she met her study group for tomorrow's exam.

Fill each blank with the correct form (past or past participle) of the verb in parentheses.

Last week, I (buy) _____ my first iPhone at the Apple store. The Apple genius had (tell) _____ me how to download apps, and I (think) _____ I had (get) _____ the idea right. But after I had (spend) _____ an hour trying to download apps, I (find) _____ it impossible, and so I (hit) _____ on the idea of calling my friend Al, who had (go) _____ to computer school. If I had (think) _____ it through more clearly, I would have (leave)_____ well enough alone, because I (forget) _____ that I had (hear) _____ that Al had (quit) _____ computer school because he had (fall) _____ in with bad company.

Anyway, after Al (come) _____ over and had (spend) _____ a few minutes with my new phone, he (tell)

_____ me that he had (catch) _____ the tip of his screw driver in the opening on the bottom of the device, and had (break) _____ the tip off inside the opening. I (find) _____ myself breathing very shallowly and I would have (weep) _____ if I had not (feel) _____ so numb. I (fight) _____ back the urge to do something rash. After I (take) _____ some deep breaths and had (spend) _____ a few seconds getting myself together, I (make) _____ the decision not to get angry because Al had not (mean) _____ any harm. After we had both (drink) _____ some nice herbal tea and I had (bring) _____ my pulse back to normal, I (say) _____ to Al that I had (feel) _____ very upset when he had first (give) _____ me the bad news. But now, after I had (weep) _____ a little inside, I (think) _____ that we could solve the problem. As long as he had not (lose) _____ the tip in the phone, everything would be fine.

Al (have) _____ an odd expression on his face. He (say) _____, "if I had (get) _____ the tip back, I would not have (spend) _____ so much time fiddling with the phone!" Al then told me that as he was fiddling with the phone, he had (cut) _____ his finger and had (bleed) _____ into the opening, which had (make) _____ the whole situation worse. As angry as I was, I (fight) _____ for control because I had (bring) _____ this on myself.

9. Upon becoming the prime minister of Britain in 1941, Winston Churchill said I have nothing to offer but blood, toil, tears, and sweat.

10. Susans constant sneezing may be the result of an allergy

11. Why is the womens restroom always more crowded than the mens?

12. In her first performance on a British talent show, Susan Boyle sang the song I Dreamed a Dream from the musical Les Miserables.

13. The neighborhoods smallest house is ours.

14. An article in the New York Times food section was titled Meeting, Then Eating, the Goat.

Part Three: Some of the following sentences contain misplaced or dangling modifiers or words that lack parallel structure. Rewrite the incorrect sentences. If a sentence has no structural errors, label it C for *correct*.

15. I hate to balance my checkbook and paying my bills.

_____

16. He not only has a black belt in judo but also in karate.

_____

17. This report must be thoroughly researched, carefully documented, and have correct organization.

_____

18. Either she will stay in the United States or return to her native country.

_____

19. The secret to success is hoping for the best but to prepare for the worst.

   _____

20. While preparing dinner, I watched the evening news on television.

   _____

21. His job was eliminated after retiring.

   _____

22. Happiness is not so much having what you want as to want what you have.

   _____

23. Before leaving for work, my children have to be dropped off at their preschool.

   _____

24. Julius Caesar summarized his actions during a battle in Turkey by saying, "I came; I saw; I conquered."

   _____

Part Four: Fill each blank with the correct form (past or past participle) of the verb in parentheses.

   Almost everyone has (hear) _____ of Romeo and Juliet, and many people have (read) _____ Shakespeare's famous play about the two lovers. The story of Romeo and Juliet was also (make) _____ into a musical called *West Side Story*, and thousands more people have (see) _____ the musical on the stage or in its movie version.

Although Shakespeare (write) _____ the play *Romeo and Juliet*, he did not create the story's plot. The story was already (know) _____ in both its original Italian and several later English versions. Romeo and Juliet (come) _____ from families (the Montagues and the Capulets) in Verona who had (be) _____ enemies for many years. The two young people (meet) _____ at a dance that was (give) _____ by Juliet's family, the Capulets. As soon as Romeo (see) _____ Juliet, he (fall) _____ in love with her. After the dance, Romeo (go) _____ back to Juliet's home and (stand) _____ in the orchard below her window. The two lovers (speak) _____ to each other and decided to get married the next day. The next day Juliet (leave) _____ her home secretly, and she and Romeo were married by Friar Lawrence.

On his way home, Romeo was (find) _____ by Juliet's cousin, Tybalt, who challenged him to a duel. Romeo (choose) _____ not to fight Tybalt, to whom he was now related by marriage. Instead, Romeo's friend Mercutio (draw) _____ his sword, (begin) _____ to fight with Tybalt, and was killed by him. Romeo then (feel) _____ that he must avenge his friend's death by killing Tybalt. After the Duke of Verona (hear) _____ about the killings, he banished Romeo to another city.

Meanwhile, Juliet had been (tell) _____ by her parents that she (have) _____ to marry another man, Paris. Friar Lawrence (think) _____ of a plan to let Juliet escape her unwanted second marriage and to be with Romeo again. The friar

(give) _____ her a sleeping potion that (make) _____ her

appear to be dead. The friar planned to revive Juliet later.

However, the letter that the friar (send) _____ to Romeo to

inform him of the plan did not reach him. When news of Juliet's supposed

death was (bring) _____ to Romeo, he (think) _____ that

she was really dead. He then (buy) _____ a poison, (go)

_____ to Juliet's tomb and (drink) _____ the poison

there.

A short time later, Juliet (wake) _____ up and (see)

_____ Romeo's dead body. Because she (feel) _____

that her life would be empty without Romeo, she killed herself.

At the end of the play, Romeo and Juliet's parents (meet)

_____ at the tomb and (say) _____ that they would

no longer be enemies.

jazz made its way into rock music, influencing jazz-rock fusion, funk and hip-hop. Without a doubt, jazz is an American music that is here to stay. Jazz, with its roots and influences bringing together so many different cultures and traditions, may truly offer a kind of universal language.

II. Controlling Principles: Unity and Coherence

Understanding the two underlying principles of paragraphs (and essays) will help you to master formal writing.

Unity

The first principle, **unity,** means *Everything in your paragraph exists to explain, describe, illustrate, prove, discuss* **one point: your topic sentence or main idea.**

Your topic sentence or main idea is the purpose of your paragraph, the reason it exists. All the sentences in your paragraph *must directly relate* to your topic sentence. If they do not, your paragraph does not have **unity,** and it will sound like a jumble of ideas.

In the exercise above, you probably were able to sense at least two paragraphs. The first few sentences all dealt with one subject: the West African roots of jazz. The main idea of that paragraph is the exercise's first sentence, "Jazz, America's most original musical art form, has its roots in West African music traditions." Every sentence in that initial paragraph *relates directly* to the topic sentence. A new subject and paragraph begin with the sentence "Jazz has given birth to a number of subgenres." The remainder of the sentences all *relate directly* to this one idea. These two paragraphs have unity.

If you decided to make the last sentence of the exercise (*"Jazz, with its roots and influences bringing together so many different cultures and traditions, may truly offer a kind of universal language"*) a new paragraph, you'd be correct. This sentence—though *indirectly* related to the previous paragraph—begins a new idea about jazz as a "universal language." It can be set off all on its own as a paragraph working as a **rhetorical unit,** or you could use it as a main idea and create a fuller, explanatory paragraph for it.

Exercise B

The following two paragraphs have problems with unity. First, identify the topic sentence or main idea of the paragraph. Then identify the problem sentences— that is, those sentences that do not *directly* relate to the topic sentence.

(1) The spring is my least favorite season. Every spring with the blooming of all those flowers, my allergies also start to bloom. We have a beautiful garden of roses, daisies, and azaleas. I wind up sneezing and coughing almost all the time. Sometimes, I get so worn out from the coughing and sneezing that I get really sick. Last spring, I wound up with a killer sinus infection. I must have taken three different antibiotics before the infection was gone. In addition, my eyes are constantly red and itchy. No amount of anti-allergy medications seems to help. Finally, the spring also gives birth to all those little insects that need to feed on me to survive! Of course, I'm allergic to bug bites, and I spend a great deal of time either scratching or looking for itch ointments! Truly, I have good reason to hate the spring.

(2) The dog we rescued this year has the sweetest temperament of any dog we have known. There are several rescue organizations in our community. Our little mutt hasn't a mean bone in his body. He seems to love everything and everybody. For example, he just loves little children. When our two-year old cousin comes over, the two of them play together like old friends. In fact, our little dog licks our cousin's face so much that we wind up laughing most of the time. This new pup also is loving towards our three elderly cats. He shares his food with them, tries to lick them too, and winds up sleeping with them in one sweet pile. He truly has a very sweet temperament.

Topic Sentences

If you can understand the purposes of a **topic sentence**, your writing will significantly improve. Determining unity becomes a relatively easy task once you are able to identify the topic sentence. You can think about the topic sentence as the seed out of which everything else grows. Or you can think of it as the picture frame that brings order and meaning to your ideas. It helps your reader (and yourself) understand what you're trying to say and makes sense of your ideas. Look at the following example of a paragraph *without* a topic sentence:

After graduating high school, your identity changes as you move from being a high school teenager to a university student or worker; your connections to home loosen as you attend school elsewhere, move to a place of your own, or simply exercise your right to stay out later.

Although you can "sense" what this paragraph is about, its meaning is *implicit*. Good academic writing makes meaning *explicit*, and this is the work of the topic sentence. Consider how much clearer the paragraph reads when we insert the following idea: "Graduating from high school is an exciting, occasionally even traumatic event." This topic sentence helps make sense of the paragraph that follows and gives you, the reader, that "aha!" experience of saying to yourself, "Oh, that's what it's all about."

The job of the topic sentence is to help make meaning explicit, clearer for the reader so he or she doesn't have to make guesses or even work too hard to figure out what he or she is reading. Experienced writers can place topic sentences in the middle or end of paragraphs, but it is better for newer writers to begin their paragraphs with the topic sentence. Your professors also expect to see paragraphs organized this way. Your textbooks generally are organized in this orderly way as well. All you need to do as you study is check off the topic sentences to know what ideas are to follow. This same experience—expectation and its fulfillment—is the basis of all strong academic writing.

However, fulfilling the expectations created by your topic sentence can be tricky. If you don't provide your reader with what is expected, your writing will not be focused and will lack unity. You can remedy much of these difficulties by identifying the **key words or controlling idea** of a topic sentence. Not only does this identification help check for paragraph unity, it also helps in the actual writing of your paragraph.

Let's look at a few examples. In the following topic sentence, ask yourself what particular words identify the sentence's main idea:

Both cable and network television have become increasingly more interactive.

What is this sentence about? Clearly, *cable and network television* and *interactive* are the key words and controlling idea of this sentence. You can probably begin to fill in the examples that might illustrate this idea. We expect this paragraph *to show us how* cable and network television have been changing. Every example needs to relate to this idea. The expectation is what the sentence is promising, committing itself to discuss.

Consider the following sentence. What are its key words and controlling idea? What do we expect to be reading about?

The economic crisis of 2009 was significantly different from earlier economic downturns.

The key words for this sentence are *economic crisis of 2009* and *significantly different*; we expect to read about *why* the 2009 crisis was so different. Here is the controlling idea; again, you might be able to provide examples and reasons to illustrate this idea. You might consider the way the use of subprime mortgages and new financial instruments like derivatives contributed to this period's economic problems. This paragraph, as the earlier one, will almost write itself— once you have identified the key words and controlling idea.

EXERCISES C

Identify the key words and controlling idea for the following sentences. Be able to state the "expectation" of the sentence—what does the paragraph to follow need to show?

1. Computer games have become America's favorite entertainment.
2. Michelle Obama has significantly changed our view of the First Lady.
3. My IPhone has made my life a lot easier.

Limit Your Topic Sentence by Asking Questions

One way to identify key words and controlling ideas in topic sentences is to ask the journalist's questions of *who? what? when? why? where?* and *how?* Quite often we find it hard to write because our main idea is unclear, too vague, or too general. Asking these questions will also help you refine and narrow your ideas.

The following topic sentence is far too *general:* "Celebrities make lots of money." If an idea is too general, it covers a large category. This sentence about "celebrities" could, for example, refer to celebrities in film or music (rock, rap, classical, jazz) or television or sports or art or politics! The category "celebrities" is too big. You might need as much as an entire essay–not a paragraph—to support this idea. Asking the question "Who?" would help narrow this very broad statement and make it more interesting, too. Here are two possible revisions: "Pop singers like the Backstreet Boys make huge amounts of money" or "Michael Jordan has made a lot of money from his celebrity." We now have a topic that is more *specific;* it is limited and precise. The next question you might ask is "What do you mean by 'huge amounts of money' and 'a lot of money'?" The paragraph about the pop singers would provide specific examples and data about CD and concert sales to show the reader how much money these performers have made; similarly, the paragraph about Michael Jordan might list examples showing how his sports, movies, and advertisement activities have made him a rich man. These two paragraphs would almost write themselves.

Being able to know as precisely as possible what it is you are trying to say will create good writing *and* make the writing itself go more smoothly.

EXERCISES D

The following topic sentences need refining. Using the "journalist's questions," rewrite each sentence. Be prepared to explain which question you used in your revision and what other questions you might ask to explain or illustrate your controlling idea.

1. Beauty pageants are interesting.

2. Studying for finals is boring.

3. Health care can be very expensive.

4. The education system has problems.

5. Sports are controversial.

Coherence

The second principle of good paragraph (and essay) writing—**coherence**—goes hand in glove with the principle of unity. Coherence means two things: (1) to cohere or stick together, and (2) to make sense logically. The opposite of coherence, then, means things have no order, make no sense, or fly off in every direction.

Certainly, having unity will remedy some coherence problems. However, even if all your sentences directly relate to your main idea, your paragraph may still be incoherent because it lacks logical relationships between its ideas. Coherence means that your paragraph has a clear structure and logical connections. As you read the paragraph below, ask yourself why it seems confused:

> Madonna's early costumes had her wearing what looked like underwear, bras, and slips. Sometimes these were worn over her clothing, sometimes all by themselves. Today, fashions for young women commonly include skirts and tops that could be undergarments. Because of changes in the way female rock performers dress, young women have been given permission to break the boundaries of what once was considered good taste. A fashion signature of singer Britney Spears is her tight clothing and bare midriff. Young girls—sometimes as young as nine years old—wear tight-fitting clothes and bear their midriffs. Fashion for young women and girls has certainly changed since the days when even a miniskirt was considered pushing the limits of taste and propriety.

This paragraph could work very well. It has general statements that provide context for its examples and a concluding closing sentence—all the components of a solid paragraph. But it is confused and incoherent; the paragraph doesn't progress logically, and its parts do not seem to "stick together" and work as a unit. Creating coherency means applying two principles: (1) providing a structural order and strategy controlling the development of the ideas, and (2) providing transitions between the ideas that create a sense of "flow" from one sentence to the next.

Let's apply these two principles to the paragraph above. First, the paragraph plunges us immediately into an example. We are disoriented because we have no idea what the example about Madonna means. *Details without a controlling statement are confusing.* The main idea of the paragraph, its topic sentence, occurs in the fourth sentence: "Because of changes in the way female performers dress, young women have been given permission to break the boundaries of what once was considered good taste." Beginning the paragraph with this idea provides a focus and context for the rest of the sentences.—We have suddenly being given a pair of glasses that allows us to see meaning and order—almost. Even with the topic sentence providing a logical context for the paragraph, it still has problems:

> Because of changes in the way female rock performers dress, young women have been given permission to break the boundaries of what once was considered good taste. Madonna's early costumes had her wearing what looked like underwear, bras, and slips. Sometimes these were worn over her clothing, sometimes all by themselves. Today, fashions for young women commonly include skirts and tops that could be undergarments. A fashion signature of singer Britney Spears is her tight clothing and bare midriff. Young girls—sometimes as young as nine years old—wear tight-fitting clothes and bear their midriffs. Fashion for young women and girls has certainly changed since the days when even a miniskirt was considered pushing the limits of taste and propriety.

After the topic sentence, the reader still has examples thrown at her or him without any preparation. Structurally, the paragraph uses the example of Madonna and Britney Spears to develop its main idea that female rock performers have radically changed fashion for young women. But we need sentences to prepare us for these examples as well as *transitions* or "bridges" between these ideas to help us see the ways they *explicitly* connect.

With only a few changes, we can significantly improve this paragraph. First, we can add two sentences that introduce Madonna and Britney Spears to the reader as examples of rock performers whose fashion sense has changed styles: "Madonna was one of the first rock performers whose clothing taste influenced the fashion scene" and "Britney Spears has also had a powerful influence on the way young women dress." These two sentences provide a bridge to each example and create a sense of logical transition. We can also signal to the reader that the last sentence is a concluding thought by inserting the evaluative term "clearly." The paragraph now reads smoothly and easily:

> Because of changes in the way female rock performers dress, young women have been given permission to break the boundaries of what once was considered good taste. Madonna was one of the first rock performers whose clothing taste influenced the fashion scene. Madonna's early costumes had her wearing what looked like underwear, bras, and

slips. Sometimes these were worn over her clothing, sometimes all by themselves. Today, fashions for young women commonly include skirts and tops that could be undergarments. Britney Spears has also had a powerful influence on the way young women dress. A fashion signature of singer Britney Spears is her tight clothing and bare midriff. Young girls sometimes as young as nine years old—wear tight-fitting clothes and bear their midriffs. Clearly, fashion for young women and girls has certainly changed since the days when even a miniskirt was considered pushing the limits of taste and propriety.

Notice that several key phrases from the topic sentence are repeated at transition points: "Madonna was one of the first *rock performers* whose clothing taste influenced the fashion scene" and "Britney Spears has also had a powerful influence on the way *young women dress*." The *repetition of key words and phrases will* create a sense of structure and order in your writing.

This exercise teaches us two other very important lessons. First, we can see how important it is to have a clear topic sentence. Second, by inserting either framing sentences or "transition" signal words, we can quickly remedy problems of coherency. Making order sometimes is as simple as adding a word or two or three. In the sentences right above, "first" and "second" are transition words that create a relationship between the sentences and, hence, a sense of order. Below are a sampling of some common transition words and phrases:

Consequence
    therefore, then, thus, hence, accordingly, as a result
Amplification
    also, again, in addition, too
Likeness and Example
    likewise, similarly, for instance, for example
Contrast
    but, however, yet, on the contrary
Sequence
    first, second, third, next, finally
Restatement
    in other words, that is
Conclusion
    in conclusion, finally, therefore, thus
Concession
    of course, it is true

By simply inserting sequence words or phrases like "for example," you can instantly create coherence *and* give your writing the feel or sophisticated formal writing.

Exercise E

Create order in the following paragraph by using the transition words and phrases listed above. You do not need to add any more sentences.

Many people believe that reading is in decline, but reading may just be changing. On July 8, 2004, the National Endowment for the Arts (NEA) published findings that showed a dramatic decline in American adults reading literature. Fewer than half were reading novels, poetry, and plays. In November 2007, the NEA reported that the number of seventeen-year olds that said they read for fun was continuing to decrease. The chairman of the NEA said that this decline in reading was a national crisis. Articles in the *New York Times* in 2008 traced the decline in reading to the increased use of the Internet. More and more teenagers are active online. They watch YouTube, check in on MySpace, Twitter, or Facebook. Some educational psychology professors think that reading is just changing. Teenagers read email and social networking messages, gain information from Google and Wikipedia, and study encyclopedia and community sites for computer games. They read online at sites like quizilla.com and fanfiction.net. Young people are reading in all sorts of ways. It just may not be very traditional.

III. Organizing Your Ideas: Structures and Strategies

Smooth transitions between sentences certainly help create order and coherence in writing. But smooth transitions cannot occur without a clear structure controlling how we arrange our ideas. Good writers are aware of ordering strategies or appropriate idea frameworks. There are many different ways to structure your writing strategically. We will look at two dominant patterns and then at three developmental strategies.

Deductive and Inductive Patterns: A Matter of Effect

At a basic level, who we are—our particular temperaments—has a lot to do with what organizing structures we choose. Some of us are detail-oriented people, and some of us come up with generalizations at the drop of a hat. Generally speaking, people for whom generalizations are easy will tend to gravitate to a **deductive development;** people who find they can easily write details will gravitate to an **inductive development.** Understanding your "writing temperament" as well as the way these two large developmental patterns work will help you be a more masterful writer.

Deductive Development: From General to Specific

We are all most familiar with deductive development, for in this structure we begin with a general idea—a topic sentence—and then use specifics in the rest of the paragraph to develop it, explain it, illustrate it, or defend it.

All the examples in this book use deductive development. Starting your paragraph with a good topic sentence (which is, as you know, a general statement of what your paragraph is about) helps the reader know what to expect.

Generalization
↓
Specifics

This is the format used most in business and academic writing because it is the easiest to read. The following paragraph is a good example of **deductive development;** the topic sentence is in italics:

> *The books included in the genre of picture books have many values in addition to pleasure.* The rhythm, rhyme, and repetition in nursery rhymes stimulate language development in young children. Alphabet books reinforce ability to identify letter/sound relationships. Concept books enhance intellectual development by fostering understanding of abstract ideas. Wordless books encourage children to develop their observational skills, descriptive vocabularies, and abilities to create stories characterized by logical sequence. Thus picture books have important roles in children's development.
>
> Donna Norton, *Through the Eyes of a Child*

The topic sentence clearly asserts its position: "The books included in the genre of picture books have many values in addition to pleasure," and we expect that the paragraph will show us in what way this statement is accurate—that is, if the paragraph performs its task well. Certainly, there are enough examples to affirm its assertion, and we accept that, yes, picture books offer many values. This structure of a generalization supported by specifics has no difficulty communicating its meaning—a good reason why it is the preferred pattern in business and education. But it is not the only way to organize ideas.

Inductive Development: From Specific to General

Another pattern inverts deductive development so that it moves from specifics to a generalization, or **inductive development**. Inductive development actually replicates the way most people think. Many of us gather information, details, and data from which we infer a generalization. Scientific method uses this type of reasoning—as do detectives in mystery stories. Consider how often Sherlock Holmes puts pieces of information together to find out the truth so that at the end of the story he can utter, "Elementary, my dear Watson." This way of organizing ideas is certainly legitimate, but notice the effect it has on your ease of comprehension in the following paragraph; the topic sentence, again, is in italics:

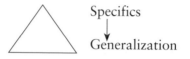

Specifics

Generalization

   With Whitaker's facts and the facts of the subscription lists before us, we seem to have arrived at three facts which are indisputable and must have great influence upon our enquiry how we can help you to prevent war. The first is that the daughters of educated men are paid very little from the public funds for their public service; the second is that they are paid nothing at all from the public funds for their private services; and the third is that their share of the husband's income is not a flesh-and-blood share but a spiritual or nominal share, which means that when both are clothed and fed, the surplus funds that can he devoted to causes, pleasures or philanthropies gravitate mysteriously but indisputably toward those causes, pleasures and philanthropies which the husband enjoys, and of which the husband approves. *It seems that the person to whom the salary is actually paid is the person who has the actual right to decide how that salary shall be spent.*

Virginia Woolf, Three Guineas

If you found this paragraph a little hard to follow, you're not alone. Once you read the last sentence, the topic sentence, the paragraph starts to make some sense; if you reread the paragraph starting with the topic sentence, then its meaning becomes substantially clearer. This paragraph, by the British novelist and essayist Virginia Woolf, isn't confusing because of its length (it is long) but because of its organization. It keeps you in suspense until its final sentence—the generalization that provides the controlling idea for the paragraph. The purpose of this kind of organization is to keep you in suspense, to keep you wondering, caught in the magic of fine language, until that final thought. However, you can see why it is a questionable pattern for situations that demand immediate clarity—as in tests, school papers, and business communication. So you can use this pattern, but be aware of its effect and use it accordingly.

This pattern, as noted above, also replicates the way many people think. You may find that you write your first drafts using inductive development. If that proves true, you can easily restructure your paragraphs by simply moving your final general idea to the beginning of the paragraph. If you are uncertain whether your paragraph has a general idea or topic sentence, check to see if it emerges at the end of your paragraphs. Although we aren't discussing essays here, the same principle applies in essay writing. Many times we "discover" our thesis or essay's purpose in our conclusion. If you are an inductive thinker, look for your main ideas in your final, concluding thoughts.

EXERCISES F

Determine whether the following paragraphs use *inductive* or *deductive* patterns of development. Be sure you underline the topic sentence of each paragraph.

1. When I started college, I thought I'd become a scientist. I've always done well in math and science courses. My sister would struggle with chemistry, but I just found it easy and even fun! When I was in high school, I was on the academic decathlon team. The teacher chose me for my science and math knowledge. I helped our team out many times by answering tricky math questions. Then I went to college. Everything changed. I had to take an English class for my general requirements. The teacher was inspiring. For the first time, I really understood poetry. I loved it and wanted more of it. Now I'm an English major, and I think I'll go on to graduate school. Life is full of surprises and the unpredictable!

*Deductive*_____ *Inductive*_____

2. My brother was laid off last month from his job at a bank. He's been looking for a job every day. He first thought he'd check out the newspapers to see what kinds of jobs were available. He found that he needed to use the Internet too, and he's signed up with Monster.Com and other job sites. He even put an ad on Craigslist to see if anyone would hire him to help do handy work. He's been going to job fairs and checking out the placement bulletin boards at his old college. I caught him yesterday calling and e-mailing old friends to see if any of

them had any leads for work. He's been able to reconnect with some old buddies. Luckily, he can live at home with us, and we admire his persistence. He's thinking about going back to school to train in an area that has more work opportunities. Although the economic downturn can be frustrating, it can also have some silver linings.

*Deductive*_____ *Inductive*_____

3. In the sixties a new sort of child appeared in motion pictures; from a sweet, idealized Shirley Temple, the movie child grew into a monster. First came a prepubescent killer in *The Bad Seed* in 1956. Then, in *Village of the Damned* (1962), sweet-faced children turned out to be malevolent beings from outer space. The trend accelerated in the late sixties and early seventies, culminating in the appearance of a spate of satanic juveniles on movie screens. *Rosemary's Baby* was the first, a mild exercise in horror compared to *The Exorcist*, which featured the first true teenage werewolf, a darling little girl transformed, at puberty, into a ravening, sexually rapacious, and murderous creature.

Marie Winn

*Deductive*_____ *Inductive*_____

4. **Now write your own paragraph:** First use *inductive structure;* after you have your inductive paragraph, make the appropriate revisions so that you re-create it in *deductive structure*. Here are some possible topic areas:

your favorite movie star	*your dream vacation*
your favorite music genre	*the chores you like least*

After you write your paragraphs, be ready to discuss how the different organizing patterns influence the communication of your ideas.

Structural Strategies: The Top Four

Whether you use a deductive or inductive pattern, your paragraph will need further structural organizing. Masterful writing is writing in which ideas have been artfully ordered. No matter how brilliant your ideas may be, if they are presented in an incoherent manner, their brilliance will be lost. Therefore, being conscious of effective organizing strategies will significantly improve your writing. Although there are many strategic ways to arrange your ideas, we're going to concentrate on what we believe are the top four formats—formats that are also most common in the academic and business arenas.

array of settings. It is easy to film almost any setting—mountains, beaches, or the inside of buildings—and use those sequences as backdrops for the action. **Live theater,** *on the contrary,* requires elaborate, hand-painted scenes. These are often very heavy and must be moved about several times during the performance. Movie directors *thus* have greater flexibility than live theater can offer in the uses of flashbacks, unspoken thoughts, and setting.

- First, the point of this comparison and contrast is clearly stated in the topic sentence: "Movie directors are able to make use of several techniques not available to directors of live theater."

- Second, the paragraph is organized around three categories: flashbacks, unspoken thoughts, and setting.

- Third, the paragraph plays Ping-Pong—it jumps back and forth between film and live theater. *There is a balance between the two discussions.* Balance is critical to good compare-and-contrast writing. The terms you use to discuss one thing, you must also use with the other.

- Notice the transition words (in italics) that indicate contrast. They not only move the ideas along but also make explicit the paragraph's intention.

Because **balance** is so important to this organizing strategy, it helps to learn the two patterns that create models for comparison and contrast writing. The paragraph above literary plays Ping-Pong—jumps back and forth between the two things being discussed. This model looks like this:

I. Category (Flashbacks)

    A. (Film)

    B. (Live Theater)

II. Category (Unspoken Thoughts)

    A. (Film)

    B. (Live Theater)

III. Category (Setting)

    A. (Film)

    B. (Live Theater)

There is another model for writing comparison and contrast; rather than playing Ping-Pong, it divides the essay in half, first discussing one item in relation to the categories and then discussing the other—again in relation to the same categories. (Remember: Balance is key to this form or writing). This model looks like this:

   I. Item (Film)

      A. Category (Flashbacks)

      B. Category (Unspoken Thoughts)

      C. Category (Setting)

  II. Item (Live Theater)

      A. Category (Flashback)

      B. Category (Unspoken Thoughts)

      C. Category (Setting)

Because you are dividing your discussion in half, a problem with this second method can occur if you forget to continue the same categories or get so tired out that you short-change the second item in your discussion.

EXERCISES G

The best way to learn to write is to write! Modeling is an excellent way to learn. In the following exercises, we will ask you to model your own paragraphs after the ones used in the discussion above.

1. Rewrite the paragraph about film and live theater using the second model.

2. Write your own comparison/contrast paragraph. First you'll need to come up with a topic area. Here are some ideas: two contrasting or similar performers, two cars, two sports players, two TV shows that are similar (for example, two reality or game or police shows). Outline your paragraph.

3. Using the classification paragraph on roommates as a model, write your own classification paragraph.

4. Write a paragraph that uses one extended example to illustrate its topic sentence.

IV. Troubleshooting

Once you have written a draft of your paragraph, the next step is to edit it. Remember: All good writing is rewriting. Read your work out loud. Listen for any problems, rough areas, moments when you pause, when the reading is hard. These areas probably have some difficulty. Paragraphs offer up their own unique difficulties. Here are some checklists to help you refine your final drafts.

1. If your writing sounds confused, unclear, check:

   - Do you have a topic sentence?
   - Do you have an organizational strategy?
   - Do you have transitions?

2. Is your paragraph too vague and general?

   - Be sure you have enough examples, details, and specifics.

3. Do you have too many details with no explicit reason for them?

   - Be sure you have a topic sentence and adequate categories.

4. Is your paragraph too long?

   - Remember how important *white space* is. We need to rest our eyes. If your paragraph runs a page or more, break it up into smaller pieces. A decent paragraph is about seven to eleven lines long.

5. Are your paragraphs too short?

   - Too many short paragraphs may be a red flag. Academic writing explains, shows, and illustrates ideas.
   - If you have very short paragraphs, check for the following possible problems:

     a. Do your paragraphs need to be developed further? Do you have enough specifics? Or,

     b. Do your short paragraphs need to be combined together under a topic sentence?

   - If all the ideas relate directly to the same general notion, then you may need to create a topic sentence and combine the paragraphs under it, or use the topic sentence you have and combine the other paragraphs.
   - Again, *generally*, academic paragraphs are about seven to eleven lines long. *But this is not a rule.* Paragraphs can be of any length. You need to be able to decide whether or not you have adequately explained your ideas.

EXERCISES G

Now consider these "troubleshooting" ideas as you review the following student paragraphs.

Consider for each:

1. Does the paragraph have a topic sentence? If so, underline it. If not, create one for the paragraph. You may first need to identify the main idea of the paragraph. What is it trying to say?

2. Does the paragraph have unity? For example, do all the sentences relate *directly* to the topic sentence? If you see any sentences that do not belong, cross them out.

3. Is the paragraph coherent? For example, does it have good transitions? Does it develop and/or illustrate its points thoroughly? Add transition words as needed. If the writer needs to develop ideas more, indicate which sentences need more development or illustration.

(1) Because many children have watched Walt Disney's film *Cinderella*, their view of stepfamilies may have been influenced by the film. Although we see that Cinderella is playing the role of a dutiful daughter and we see the importance of family, we develop a negative connotation of the idea of a stepfamily. "In films depicting stepfamilies, all of the stepmothers are portrayed as evil" (Tanner 367). Many children may have actually gone through a situation similar to Cinderella's, such as losing a parent and having their parent remarry or having a divorced parent remarry. It automatically makes the children see the new member of the family in a negative light. The children may be constantly reminded of what the stepfamily in Cinderella was like, and this will make it harder for them to be more accepting of their new family situation.

(2) Shel Silverstein's poetry for children is often silly, humorous, and a little strange. Silverstein illustrated his own books with black-and-white line drawings. The accompanying black-and-white illustrations, amusing and sometimes rather morbid, are an integral part of the poetry. The illustrations are often needed in order to interpret the poem itself. Silverstein believed that written works needed to be read on paper—the correct paper for the particular work. He usually would not allow his poems and stories to be published unless he could choose the type, size, shape, color, and quality of the paper himself. Being a book collector himself, he took seriously the feel of paper, the look of the book from the inside and out, the typeface for each poem, and the binding of his books. He did not allow his books to be published in paperback because he did not want his work to diminish in any way.

Answers to "A" Exercises

Exercise 1A

1. hunger is
2. Malnutrition kills
3. product has
4. name is
5. Plumpynut contains
6. Plumpynut is
7. It comes
8. mothers squeeze
9. children lose
10. they love
11. advantage is
12. Feeding costs
13. children recover
14. gain is
15. groups build
16. Mothers come
17. personnel weigh
18. They monitor
19. patients appear
20. children go
21. They return
22. mothers continue
23. Plumpynut is
24. nations produce
25. factories provide
26. They give

Exercise 2A

1. story is
2. It seems / women obeyed
3. town had
4. mayor did / everyone respected
5. man had

6. He was
7. wife nagged scolded
8. he was / he had
9. mayor decided
10. He called
11. men came seated
12. mayor separated
13. He told / men went
14. men moved / man moved
15. mayor husbands stared
16. he had / they wanted
17. man seemed / he spoke
18. I know / I came
19. I sat / wife tells

Exercise 3A

1. cave contains
2. daughter discovered
3. name was
4. father searched / Maria wandered
5. she noticed
6. Maria was
7. Altamira became
8. Drawings cover
9. handprints appear
10. artists painted
11. shape follows
12. Using gives
13. Historians call
14. government had
15. Warmth allowed
16. fungus threatened
17. visitors wanted
18. solution was
19. replica allows
20. you have / (you) try

Exercise 4A

1. people need / salt has played
2. humans hunted / meat provided
3. people began / they needed
4. Salt can be extracted / it can be mined
5. salt was / it became
6. salt was used
7. Greeks could purchase
8. slave was described / we hear
9. soldiers received
10. payment was called / it is
11. salt was / governments taxed
12. emperors levied / government collected
13. Mahatma Gandhi led
14. kings sold / salt became
15. scarcity was
16. price became
17. salt was used
18. People learned
19. restaurants stores offer
20. people must limit
21. markets sell
22. we need / it continues

Exercise 5A

1. spend
2. accounts
3. is
4. were
5. include
6. are
7. live
8. are
9. include
10. covers
11. does

12. is
13. makes
14. provides
15. has
16. comes
17. help
18. is
19. is
20. prevents
21. are
22. costs

Exercise 6A

1. needs
2. offers
3. plan
4. have
5. Has
6. offers
7. are
8. comes
9. is
10. has
11. C
12. makes
13. is
14. determines
15. gathers
16. C
17. is
18. C
19. is
20. was
21. C
22. needs
23. agrees
24. is
25. is

Exercise 7A

1. makes
2. is
3. seems
4. kills
5. has
6. is
7. studies
8. summarizes
9. is
10. is
11. is
12. is
13. charge
14. gives
15. rents
16. is
17. fall
18. advises
19. outweigh
20. comes
21. is
22. makes
23. are
24. is
25. requires
26. appeals

Exercise 8A

1. are
2. adds
3. belongs
4. needs
5. agrees
6. has
7. Is

8. comes
9. is
10. Have
11. lie
12. know
13. needs
14. allows
15. is
16. comes
17. has
18. flies
19. needs
20. costs
21. is
22. is
23. Does
24. comes
25. Has

Exercise 9A

1. VIII, so
2. wives, for
3. Aragon; she
4. brother; however, he
5. children; nevertheless, only
6. throne, and
7. wife; otherwise, he
8. divorce; therefore, Henry
9. C
10. marriage, but
11. son; however, this
12. wife, so
13. executed; thus, Henry
14. C
15. political; he
16. marriage, and
17. Anne; he

18. consummated; consequently, it
19. wife, and
20. treason; therefore, Henry
21. wife, for
22. twice, so
23. Henry, nor
24. C
25. 1547, yet
26. time; however, she
27. remember, so

Exercise 10A

1. Although few people have heard of Joseph Glidden,
2. When Americans think of the Old West,
3. after large numbers of farmers and ranchers began to settle on the plains. C
4. so that they could mark the boundaries of their property and protect their livestock and their crops. C
5. Unless their land was fenced,
6. until they built fences. C
7. When people in other parts of the United States built fences,
8. Because the West had a very limited supply of trees and large rocks,
9. Although they tried to raise thorny hedges for fences,
10. because a single strand of wire was not strong enough to restrain a herd of animals on the run. C
11. when Joseph Glidden invented barbed wire in 1874. C
12. because it had sharp steel barbs. C
13. Even though animals often tried to break through ordinary wire fences,
14. so that he could sell it at a cheap price. C
15. Because settlers now had an effective and inexpensive way to fence their land,
16. Wherever there were barbed-wire fences,
17. After he invented barbed wire,
18. When he died,
19. If you travel to the city of LaCrosse, Kansas,
20. While you are at the museum,
21. as though you were back on a cattle ranch in the Old West. C
22. If Joseph Glidden were alive today,

Exercise 11A

Corrections will vary. The following are possible answers.

1. immigrants, and each
2. Although Americans . . . countries, some
3. examples, for few
4. "frankfurters" because the
5. German), so another
6. steak," but it
7. beef; however, other
8. chop suey; this
9. laborers, but it
10. Although Americans . . . Mexican, American-style
11. food because it
12. toppings; however, pizza
13. dish, but in
14. bread; it
15. pocket, so this
16. Because the . . . pocket), people
17. Although Americans . . . countries, American
18. C

Exercise 12A

Corrections will vary. The following are possible answers.

Paragraph 1
        When you were a child, did your mother
        Carrots are among

Paragraph 2
        Although carrots are orange now, the original
        They quickly replaced the older purple carrots because
        purple

Paragraph 3
>Carrots were valued
>A single carrot contains more
>Carrots are also

Paragraph 4
>If you eat too many carrots, your skin
>This condition is physically harmless although it is
>They fed carrots to their cattle to produce
>Housewives borrowed this trick and added

Paragraph 5
>Although it may seem strange, carrots used to be eaten mainly as desserts in pies

Exercise 13A

1. sleep, don't
2. However, many
3. On the whole, doctors
4. Nevertheless, many
5. health; in fact, it
6. concentrate; for example, sleep-deprived
7. gain; therefore, if
8. diabetes; furthermore, it
9. adults; in fact, they
10. Of course,
    social activities, etc.
11. adults; in addition, research
12. problem; therefore, they
13. deprivation, for example, time
14. city; thus, many
15. California, for instance, commuters
16. Furthermore, these
17. Of course, leaving
18. In addition, sleepy
19. sleep-deprived; in fact, they

20. closes; after all, they
21. Well, someone
22. family, isn't it?
23. C
24. However, I

Exercise 14A

1. Thorpe, the most
2. Indian, a member
3. Americans, the Carlisle
4. hands, the kind of jobs
5. sports, football and track
6. Warner, the founder
7. awards, membership
8. events, the pentathlon and the decathlon
9. year, 1913, the International
10. athlete, a person
11. medals, professional baseball, and played
12. season, the best season of his entire career, Thorpe
13. feat, hitting
14. wall, his first
15. homer, an inside-the-ballpark home run, was
16. Association, the forerunner
17. play, kicking
18. honor, best
19. career, the loss of his 1912 gold medals, was
20. honor, selection

Exercise 15A

1. (author) who was world-famous a generation or two ago C
2. (Pearl Buck,) who was the first American woman to win the Nobel Prize for literature.
3. (The Good Earth,) which describes the life of a farmer in a Chinese village.

4. (China,) where her parents were Presbyterian missionaries.
5. (foreigners) who lived there. C
6. (Randolph-Macon Woman's College,) which was located in Virginia.
7. (man) who was an agricultural economist. C
8. (techniques) that would improve their productivity. C
9. (material) . . . that she would use in many of her later novels. C
10. (stories) and (essays) that were published in leading American magazines, like *The Nation* and the *Atlantic Monthly*. C
11. (East Wind, West Wind,) which told the story of a traditional Chinese woman
    (woman) who learns about Western civilization
    (doctor) who was educated in the United States
12. (Richard Walsh,) who worked at John Day, would
13. (The Good Earth,) which established her reputation as a writer, became
14. (Pulitzer Prize,) which is awarded each year for the best American works of literature.
15. (Wang Lung,) who begins his adult life as a small village farmer but eventually becomes a wealthy landowner.
16. (movie) that appeared in 1937. C
17. (actors) who were European. C
18. (make-up) that made them look somewhat Asian. C
19. (Luise Rainer,) who played the role of O-Lan, studied
    (woman) who had been hired as an extra on the set.
20. (Buck,) who watched part of the filming.
21. (Motion Picture Academy,) which gave Rainer an Oscar for best actress in 1937.
22. (Nobel Prize,) which is the highest award
    (award) that an author can receive
23. (readers) who preferred to read Chinese authors writing about their own country.
24. (students) whose first knowledge of Chinese life came from reading this novel in their English classes. C
25. (event) that put *The Good Earth* back on the best-seller list for the first time since 1932. C
26. (Oprah Winfrey,) who made it a selection of her book club.
27. (Viewers) who watched Oprah's television show C
28. (woman) who is one of television's most important personalities C

Exercise 16A

Note: The comma before the final item in a series is optional.

1. Monday, June 7, through Sunday, June 13, the . . . Orlando, Florida
2. C
3. vacation, the children
4. sites, reading travel brochures, and listening
5. money, the children's
6. members, free shuttle rides . . . Studios, and a kitchenette
7. Road, Orlando, Florida
8. Baltimore, Maryland, instead
9. Florida, they . . . Virginia, to look at furniture outlets in North Carolina, and to visit
10. places, to have lots of fun together, and to create
11. 2009, the United
12. May 16, 2009, the Associated
13. stew, canned chili, and Spam
14. inexpensive, filling, and easy
15. reasons, Kraft
16. conditions, consumers
17. remedies, antacids, and laxatives
18. Company, more
19. C
20. Avenue, Warminster, Pennsylvania

Exercise 17A

1. We should phone you
2. I have known them
3. He hired her
4. She invited us
5. They need to see you
6. I ate dinner with him
7. he

8. me
9. We
10. she
11. me
12. us
13. she
14. us
15. him
16. us
17. her
18. me
19. she
20. they

Exercise 18A

1. he
2. I
3. I
4. her
5. us
6. themselves
7. than he
8. between you and me
9. by my roommate and me
10. C
11. daughter still lives (no *she*)
12. than he
13. it is she
14. told the captain and me
15. ourselves
16. We council members
17. C
18. Susan and we
19. to them and us
20. Matthew and I

Exercise 19A

1. his
2. its
3. they
4. his
5. her
6. his or her
7. her
8. their
9. his
10. she . . . her
11. his or her medical care
12. than I
13. C
14. my husband and me
15. We parents
16. her and her assistant
17. Judy and me
18. themselves
19. Our neighbors and we
20. it is we
21. driver and me
22. between you and me

Exercise 20A

1. Who's
2. C
3. they're
4. its
5. whose
6. your supervisor if you're
7. ours
8. My husband and I
9. Yours

10. It's
11. It's
12. than I
13. sister and I
14. her job, she may also lose her health insurance
15. their father and me
16. It is we
17. We senior citizens
18. C
19. than I
20. he or she must have

Exercise 21A

1. James A. Michener *Hawaii The Source Tales of the South Pacific* Pulitzer Prize
2. Aunt Sarah Uncle Bob Houston Texas
3. The Hillcrest Medical Clinic Springfield Missouri Doctor Paul Anderson
4. San Francisco's Fairmont Hotel Mason Street Nob Hill
5. In Spanish Spain Basque Catalan Galician
6. Honolulu I Bishop Museum University of Hawaii Pearl Harbor Iolani Palace
7. Christmas Thanksgiving Memorial Day Fourth of July
8. Our March April
9. Illinois Pacific Northwest
10. French Charles River
11. Mom Dad's
12. Kraft Campbell's
13. This Maria Math American
14. Italian Renaissance Michelangelo Raphael
15. More Civil War Gettysburg
16. One Robert Frost's "Stopping by Woods on a Snowy Evening"
17. Swedish Midwest World War One
18. The John Steinbeck's *Of Mice and Men* Academy Award
19. Monday April Harper Hospital Detroit Michigan
20. Empire State Building *Sleepless in Seattle*

Exercise 22A

1. me – the biggest surprise of my entire life – was
2. said, "The only . . . itself."
3. tall, frosty
4. you: your
5. daughter-in-law's children's
6. baby's
7. students'
8. O'Connor's "A Good Man Is Hard to Find," author's
9. said, "Balancing our state's . . . all of us."
10. "We must realize," added the governor, "that failing . . . future."
11. "Does . . . year?" asked
12. Olsen's "I Stand Here Ironing"?
13. Shakespeare's *Romeo and Juliet West Side Story*
14. "If I Had a Hammer"; it '60s
15. women's couldn't
16. B.A.'s
17. Everybody's
18. quarter's
19. cool, shady
20. Isn't year's
21. Pavarotti's "Nessun Dorma" *Turandot*
22. *Time* "Rebuilding the Middle Kingdom" China's
23. here – and that means every one of you – by
24. They're wife's aren't
25. "The Star-Spangled Banner"!

Exercise 23A

Answers will vary. The following are possible corrections.

1. Henry gave his wife flowers purchased at the supermarket.
2. while he waited for the results of the exam.
3. evening, George had trouble focusing his eyes.
4. The salesperson showed the customer the coat that was on sale . . .
5. After I spent six months in Mexico, my Spanish . . .

6. She served her guests wine that . . .
7. When I was sixteen, my father bought . . .
8. C
9. She exchanged her dollars for francs in a French bank.
10. From 5 to 6 P.M., the restaurant offers . . .
11–15: Answers will vary.

Exercise 24A

Answers will vary. The following are possible corrections. The words in parentheses may be omitted.

1. to pull over to the curb and (to) show him my driver's license
2. ask to be given either liberty or death?
3. for exercising and (for) doing volunteer work
4. has not only a swimming pool but also a hot tub
5. to speak politely to the guests and (to) smile
6. tasty, nutritious, and inexpensive
7. parallel structure, punctuation, and capitalization
8. C
9. competent, experienced, and enthusiastic
10. and that help me to understand my world better
11–15: Answers will vary.

Exercise 25A

1. seen
2. thought left
3. bought worn
4. paid lost
5. drank went
6. swore broke
7. meant drove
8. caught lost
9. hurt broken
10. spoken chosen

11. grown begun
12. heard
13. ate
14. found
15. gave
16. kept
17. sold spent
18. taught
19. grown brought
20. eaten paid
21. hurt
22. hit
23. left lay seen
24. taken found had broken
25. spent gave
26. found told
27. wept spoke
28. slept kept
29. taken
30. come brought
31. done lent
32. meant begun

Exercise 26A

The answers to this exercise are on page 297 in the section titled "Unity."

INDEX